An Unexpected Journey

Other books by J. Philip Wogaman published by Westminster John Knox Press

Christian Moral Judgment

Christian Ethics: A Historical Introduction

Readings in Christian Ethics: A Historical Sourcebook (J. Philip Wogaman and Douglas M. Strong, editors)

From the Eye of the Storm: A Pastor to the President Speaks Out

Speaking the Truth in Love: Prophetic Preaching to a Broken World

Christian Perspectives on Politics (Revised and Expanded)

An Unexpected Journey

Reflections on Pastoral Ministry

J. Philip Wogaman

Westminster John Knox Press
LOUISVILLE • LONDON

Book design by Sharon Adams
Cover design by Eric Walljasper, Minneapolis, MN
Cover photograph courtesy of Paul Hosefros/New York Times Photo

First edition
Published by Westminster John Knox Press
Louisville, Kentucky

This book is printed on acid-free paper that meets the American National Standards Institute Z39.48 standard. ♾

PRINTED IN THE UNITED STATES OF AMERICA

04 05 06 07 08 09 10 11 12 13—10 9 8 7 6 5 4 3 2 1

Library of Congress Cataloging-in-Publication Data

Wogaman, J. Philip.
An unexpected journey : reflections on pastoral ministry / J. Philip Wogaman—1st ed.
p. cm.
Includes bibliographical references.
ISBN 0-664-22585-3 (alk. paper)
1. Wogaman, J. Philip. 2. United Methodist Church (U.S.)—Washington (D.C.)—Clergy—Biography. 3. Methodist Church—Washington (D.C.)—Clergy—Biography. I. Title.

BX8495.W67A3 2004
253—dc22 2003064504

TO CAROLYN

who shared the journey

Contents

Foreword

Pastoral ministry is one of the few generalist vocations remaining in a society of specialists. Pastors are called upon to serve as priests, preachers, theologians,ethicists, counselors, educators, social workers, business administrators, personnel directors, fund-raisers, community organizers, politicians, and media experts. Pastoral ministry is, indeed, a challenging and demanding vocation.

The public image of pastors seems to have diminished over the last several decades. Once the most educated and prominent persons in most communities, pastors now minister to and with parishioners who have far more education and public prominence than they. The images of pastors often portrayed in public media are less than flattering. Clergy are frequently seen as naive, ill-informed, superficial, moralistic, and even morally suspect.

Yet clergy are uniquely poised as change agents and contributors to the common good. They speak to millions of people every Sunday and are looked to for guidance on the most crucial matters facing persons and communities. Pastors are confronted daily with opportunities for comforting the grieving, encouraging the defeated, guiding the confused, strengthening the weak, nurturing community, addressing societal problems, and connecting people with God.

Little wonder pastors can lack confidence and assurance. The complexity of everyday problems and challenges, the sheer number and breadth of the pastoral demands, and the absence of public affirmation create insecurity for even the most competent pastors. Doubts arise as to the value of what they do and their own ability to fulfill their calling.

Today's pastors need mentors and role models who understand their plight and share their struggles, colleagues from whom they can learn and be inspired. J. Philip Wogaman provides such a resource. Although few pastors are placed in the extraordinary circumstance of having the president and first family as parishioners, the challenges and routines of Dr. Wogaman's years as pastor of Foundry United Methodist Church provide rich insight into ministry in less dramatic settings.

An Unexpected Journey is one pastor's journey that has implications for all pastors' journeys. Every pastor could, and perhaps should, write a similar account of his or her journey. In this way we could all learn from one another. Dr. Wogaman's journey contains many unique twists and turns: from an academic scholar and administrator to a local church pastor at age sixty, succeeding a revered pastor of twenty-seven years who subsequently confessed to boundary violations with members of the congregation; serving as pastor to the president and his family, a president who confessed to sexual misconduct with a White House intern; coping with national and international media attention.

The dramatic and extraordinary components of Dr. Wogaman's pastoral journey, however, reveal qualities necessary for faithful ministry amid routine and ordinary circumstances. Dr. Wogaman's training and experience as a theologian and ethicist uniquely equipped him to deal with the ethical and moral complexities he confronted as the pastor of President Clinton. But every pastor must be a serious theologian and ethicist in order to minister to ordinary people confronting everyday decisions and challenges.

Dr. Wogaman's pastoral journey was fraught with numerous temptations to personal aggrandizement, opportunism, and vindictiveness. Yet his strong personal and professional integrity and clear understanding of and focus on the pastoral role enabled him to remain truthful, prophetic, and compassionate. Every pastor confronts the lure of applause and the devastation of criticism. Personal identity anchored in God's grace and vocational focus on sharing in God's ministry of reconciliation and transformation are necessary if pastors are to remain faithful amid the temptations of applause and criticism.

Although Dr. Wogaman's role as pastor of a prominent church with prestigious members in extraordinary circumstances provides the backdrop and theme for *An Unexpected Journey*, the dominant story lies beyond the newsworthy. Dr. Wogaman spent most of his time and energy visiting the sick, comforting the bereaved, encouraging the defeated, seeking out the lonely, reconciling the estranged—those whose names few would recognize or remember. Such is the privilege of all pastors. Treating all people with respect and dignity and grace, whether the president of the

United States or the unnamed mother of a son dying of AIDS—that is the model of pastoral ministry.

I have known Dr. Wogaman as a seminary professor and dean, a denominational leader, a scholar and teacher, an advocate for justice and compassion, as a local church pastor, and as a friend. Although *An Unexpected Journey* chronicles his experiences as pastor of Foundry United Methodist Church, his pastoral journey encompasses his entire life. He has approached every role, whether in the academy or the church or in the broader society, as a pastor. His pastoral journey, therefore, encourages us all, laity and clergy, to continue our journey with faithfulness, thanksgiving, and joy.

Kenneth L. Carder, Bishop
Mississippi Area
The United Methodist Church

Preface

James Wall, then editor of *The Christian Century*, first suggested that I consider writing a memoir of my experience as senior minister of Foundry United Methodist Church in Washington, D.C. He thought there would be interest in my move from a quarter century as a seminary professor to service at that historic church. The interest would be compounded by the fact that the president of the United States and the first lady had become regular attendees at the church. Jim offered advice about the tone that such a book should have, a mark I could have achieved, however, only if I had his gifts as a writer! Nevertheless, the thought of such a book intrigued me, and I kept it in the back of my head throughout the ten years I served at Foundry.

Those years proved to be adventurous beyond any of my own expectations. I had to learn what it means to be a caring pastor and to preach regularly to a diverse and alert congregation. I faced routine problems of administration that would be familiar to every pastor, but there were other things. I was pastor to a church confronting the revelation that a revered senior minister had crossed boundaries "of a sexual nature" in pastoral situations, then there was the long process of deciding whether to become a Reconciling Congregation (in United Methodist parlance that is one that is specifically open to gay and lesbian Christians), then there was the president's association with the church, which brought unusual attention to the church—from the press, from visitors, from hostile demonstrators. Additionally, there were the extraordinary challenges brought on by the presidential crisis of 1998–99, some of which could have been anticipated, but much of which could not. A clergy colleague once remarked that what he appreciated about ministry was the fact that every day is unique in its challenges and opportunities, and that was certainly true for me. In retrospect, my wife, Carolyn, and I wouldn't trade anything for the ten years we served this remarkable church, even though, as the title suggests, so much of this was unexpected.

Jack Keller, editorial director at Westminster John Knox Press, visualized this book as an invitation to clergy and seminary students to "look over my shoulder," observing how I faced various problems and challenges in ministry. I'm sure he didn't mean by that to suggest that I always faced those problems and challenges in an exemplary way! We can learn from one another's mistakes as well as from the successes. Perhaps a memoir of this kind can offer something of the "feel" of pastoral ministry, particularly since it offers a fresh perspective from one who spent many years as a professor of Christian ethics. A clergy colleague who read the manuscript remarked that it helped her revisit her own ministry, different though it has been from mine. I will be very pleased if clergy colleagues find the book useful in that way and if they find their own very different pastoral journeys affirmed.

Of course, ministry is not just for clergy! I will also be very pleased if lay Christians are helped by this book to gain a better sense of the church as a whole and what it looks like from a perspective of pastoral leadership. I have learned more from lay Christians than I could possibly acknowledge in one book, although I hope some of what I have learned is reflected here. We are all on a journey together, and we learn from one another. I do not know whether the book will find readers from beyond the Christian community. I will be very happy if it does. I believe that God is bigger than any of us and that God's grace is showered upon all of us. Perhaps the book will give some small insight into what the Christian church feels like to one privileged to serve as a pastor and that that may deepen the sensitivity of the adherents of non-Christian faiths to their own traditions and communities.

My own decision to seek ordination came at a church youth camp many years ago in the Chiricahua Mountains of southern Arizona. I had just finished high school. Looking back upon the decision half a century later, I marvel at its immaturity! Yet it became the basis of spiritual growth and accumulating insight through the years. I had originally planned to serve local churches as a pastor through my entire ministry. As it turned out, I was led to pursue a doctorate in social ethics and then to exercise my ministry as a professor—for five years at the University of the Pacific, then for twenty-six years at Wesley Theological Seminary. Only in 1992, after I had turned sixty, did I become a local church pastor. While my journey really began in the 1950s, this book is primarily about the ten years at Foundry Church.

I have sought to tell the story honestly, but it is not possible to relate everything. That is partly because so many things happened during those years, but it is also because I must not break the trust of pastoral confidences. In some instances, I have sought and gained permission to record what would otherwise have to remain confidential, and in other cases I comment on matters that were already quite public within and beyond the Foundry congregation. Most of the pastoral stories during those years, told and untold, are about how God's grace has been expressed through the lives of really fine people from whom I have learned much. The book is partly chronological, but it seemed best to me to highlight certain aspects of my Foundry experience in separate chapters. I have prefaced each chapter with a brief characterization of what is to follow, using a late-Victorian literary device that one seldom encounters anymore. I hope this will help draw the reader into the chapter.

In writing this book, I owe much to many people—most of all to the people of Foundry. What good friends they turned out to be! My greatest regret in writing the book is that it is quite impossible to tell the story of my relationship with each of them and what I have gained from them. The book itself has been improved by the critical reading of several colleagues in ministry who, from their own different perspectives, were kind enough to reflect upon mine. While thanking the Revs. Evans Crawford, William Holmes, and Mary Kraus, and Bishops Kenneth Carder and Joseph Yeakel for this service, they are of course to be absolved of any responsibility for the book's remaining shortcomings. I value Bishop Carder's contribution of a foreword to the book more than I can say. This volume, like a couple of my previous books, has been much improved by the careful editorial comments of my Westminster John Knox Press editor, Stephanie Egnotovich.

I have dedicated this work to my wife, Carolyn, also an indispensable reader and critic of the book. Much more than that, we have been on this journey together, every step of the way. Neither of us has regretted our decision to take up a ministry at Foundry, and we celebrate it together.

Chapter One

Beginnings

In which I am lured away from a seminary professorship to become a pastor—meet a very surprised church committee—face the challenges of regular preaching to a diverse congregation—lose an election for bishop

I don't even remember what I was doing when the call came. It was a Monday evening, February 10, 1992. My wife, Carolyn, was attending a meeting. I was seated on the sofa in the living room, perhaps reading, possibly watching television, maybe just daydreaming, when the phone rang.

It was the Rev. Mary Brown Oliver, district superintendent of the Washington Central District. A district superintendent in the United Methodist Church is a kind of subbishop, a part of the bishop's cabinet, with oversight responsibility for sixty or seventy churches. Mary was a friend, but as a seminary professor I was not one of her pastors. Why was she calling?

"Phil," she began, "the bishop and cabinet wonder whether you would consider a major career change." Please, she added, "don't say no until you hear me out." So I listened. Would I be willing to leave my faculty position at Wesley Theological Seminary to become senior minister of Foundry United Methodist Church in downtown Washington, D.C., she asked. I already knew that Dr. Edward W. Bauman was due to retire from Foundry in a few months, after a highly successful pastorate of more than twenty-seven years, which included a well-regarded radio and television ministry. I was fairly well acquainted with Ed and Foundry since Wesley Seminary is in the same city and Ed had occasionally taught a course there.

I asked Mary every question I could think of. I was not being invited to be a candidate—I was being offered the job. In the United Methodist Church the bishop, on advice of the cabinet and in consultation with church and pastor, has the power to make appointments. Sometimes, in the case of large influential churches, a bishop will go along with the decision of a church's search committee. That wasn't to be the case here. While one can debate the relative merits of that method of pastoral appointment versus a congregational system, United Methodist church law calls for a bishop to make appointments. It certainly made it easier for me. I would not have been willing to go through a candidacy process and all that it would entail. I had been a professor of Christian ethics at Wesley for twenty-six years, eleven of them as dean of the seminary. It had been a wonderful life. I loved teaching and writing books in my field of Christian ethics, and I had many opportunities to be a church leader. At the time, I was chair of the Conference Board of Ordained Ministry, the body that supervises candidates for ordination and handles other clergy-relationship functions, and I was about to be a second-term delegate to the denomination's governing body, the General Conference. Moreover, I had just been proposed by our delegation for election as bishop. No, I would not have considered a candidacy for this or any other pastorate.

Still, I found the invitation very attractive. Please think it over, Mary said. I promised I would.

A few minutes later Carolyn popped in. "Honey," I said, "let's take a walk. There's something we have to talk about." She was as interested in the prospect as I was. After sixteen years as a preschool teacher, she had already decided to retire in order to devote her energies to inner-city projects and programs on a voluntary basis. In the center of Washington, Foundry had a number of strong mission groups dealing with the needs and problems of inner-city people. Our going to Foundry would be attractive to her. We talked far into the night. Still, we needed to know more about what this might mean.

The next day I called another friend on the bishop's cabinet. "Jean," I wanted to know, "when Ed Bauman leaves Foundry after twenty-seven years, how much of the congregation will also leave?" "Frankly," she replied, "we don't know!" Nevertheless, she urged me to say yes and assured me that if I did the bishop and cabinet would back me up even if the church had to be scaled back considerably. Her appraisal was comforting in one sense, disquieting in another.

For nineteen years our family had attended the large Metropolitan Memorial United Methodist Church near the seminary, and its pastor, Bill

Holmes, was a good friend and confidant. I sounded him out on what it's really like to be senior minister of such a church and asked what he knew about Foundry. He had helpful comments to make about both questions, but he was more interested in my being elected bishop. Would my going to Foundry help or hurt that prospect? We explored that together, inconclusively.

I talked next with a faculty colleague who was an active leader in the Foundry congregation. Ellis had only positive things to say about the church. And so, back home, I sat down to formulate one of those lists of pros and cons. To provide musical background, I put on a CD of Foundry's superb choir. That in itself was almost enough!

Then it was time for us to talk to the bishop, Joseph Yeakel. Carolyn and I made an appointment to see him the next day. Joe and I are good friends, and in my capacity as chair of the Board of Ordained Ministry, we had faced a number of problems together. Now he appealed to me directly. Foundry was going to be facing a crisis. He had already dropped hints of a possible clergy scandal at the church that could explode in the media. In any case, the departure of a nationally famous pastor could be very destabilizing. Foundry was located in the heart of the nation's capital. It was historic. It was influential. The denomination had a great stake in its continued vitality. I could do it, he assured me.

Well, could I? I was vain enough to think so and naive enough not to know what it would really mean to make such a career change. Still, after twenty-six years of seminary teaching (and previously five years at a West Coast university), the change might be interesting. In any case, I was about to turn sixty. At that age, what could be all that intimidating even if the bishop's generous appraisal of my abilities turned out to be mistaken?

There remained, however, the upcoming election for bishop. I was frankly more interested in that than in the position at Foundry, doubtless for all the wrong reasons. Well, Joe said, when anybody is elected bishop that call has to preempt everything else. I'm not sure that is quite so, but I wouldn't have wanted to accept the pastorate without being clear that I was not going to issue a Shermanesque renunciation of a possible election. The conversation turned to deeper sharing about the calling we all have from God. The bishop said that he had felt led to ask us to go to Foundry. Carolyn and I looked at each other. We also felt led to accept, we said. We all joined our hands in prayer. Only two days had elapsed since Mary's call. In the ten years since, neither Carolyn nor I have had a moment of doubt that it was the right decision, not even when faced with problems we never could have anticipated that day in the bishop's office.

With a flair for the dramatic, Rev. Oliver laid out the process of announcement. She would summon Foundry's Staff-Parish Relations Committee to a meeting at 7:30 P.M. on February 25. Carolyn and I were to present ourselves at the church entrance at 7:45. Upon our arrival, Mary ushered us into the conference room. Opening the door with a flourish, she presented me as "your new senior minister." Such a procedure certainly heightened the contrast between our appointment system and that of more congregationally based denominations.

I already knew two of the people there quite well: Dr. Walter Shropshire, a former ethics student of mine who would be a pastoral colleague at the church, and Cindy Strong, the wife of seminary colleague Dr. Douglas Strong. They were, of course, appropriately shocked, as were others present who knew who I was. Nevertheless, we had a splendid conversation. Carolyn and I were asked about our background and about issues facing the church, then we asked our own questions in turn. Some of the members knew I was being proposed for bishop, and I tried to be clear that if I was elected, somebody else would have to become their senior minister. The group's response, both during and after the meeting, was warmly positive. One member wrote to say that there had been a good deal of resentment about the appointment process, but that it had all dissipated by the way the process had turned out.

In retrospect, I think I would have wanted the Staff-Parish Committee to have been sounded out quietly in advance. I still wouldn't have been a candidate as such, but neither would I have wanted to begin a pastorate where the people had serious reservations. As it turned out, they didn't seem to anyway. Regardless of the system of church government, these decisions can be quite stressful for both clergy and laypersons. The pastoral role is very important in the life of a congregation, even central in many respects. Prospective pastors should not aspire to serve churches where they simply could not serve effectively, regardless of external factors such as prestige or material rewards. The wise counsel of others can be helpful. In the end, of course, there has to be a pretty high trust level that things will work out—and a commitment to do the best we can.

In the weeks that followed, after public announcement was made, I was frequently asked why I would ever leave a seminary faculty post to become a pastor. My flip answer to that was that after twenty-six years of helping to educate future pastors, it was my turn to put up or shut up. Carolyn's response was that it had just taken me longer to get out of seminary than most people. We love the seminary, and it has in fact been possible for me to continue to do some teaching. But the change gave us both a new burst of energy.

Preparation

I had about four months to prepare for my new responsibilities, which would begin July 1. That spring I was on sabbatical leave from the seminary and was writing a history of Christian ethics. I was also to be a delegate to the General Conference of our denomination in early May. I took these responsibilities seriously, but I also had to prepare for Foundry. Walt Shropshire, who was to become my colleague, was immensely helpful in providing background on the church and keeping me up-to-date on its current developments. I discovered to my delight that Homer Calkins had written a 350-page history of the church, tracing it from its origins in 1814 to 1965.[1]

I read that history avidly and with deepening appreciation for the historic significance of the church. Parts of the church's story are colorful. One of the early pastors—through a memorable sermon to the U.S. House of Representatives—played a key role in getting the practice of dueling banned. That was after a congressman had been shot dead in a duel with one of his colleagues. Then there was the role of Foundry representatives in petitioning the Baltimore Conference to prohibit use of chewing tobacco in church. It seems that the floors were becoming slippery underfoot, making it difficult for worshipers to get down on their knees for prayer in the usual manner. Even the pulpit was getting stained. On a more serious note, members of the church were apparently on both sides of the slavery question. At one time more than half were African Americans, but they were treated with disrespect and withdrew to form a separate church in the 1830s.

The name *Foundry* was itself acquired in a colorful way. In 1814, during the War of 1812, British troops threatened Washington. A prominent Methodist, Henry Foxall, owned a substantial metal foundry in Georgetown. Since the foundry was a principal supplier of military hardware for the federal government, Foxall concluded that it would be a likely target for British attack. He addressed the problem to God in prayer, vowing that if his foundry should be spared he would provide the money to build a new Methodist chapel in the central part of Washington. Sure enough, a summer squall drenched the British troops and flooded Rock Creek, rendering access to Georgetown difficult. That, and the death of several of the British in a munitions accident, forced a change of plans. After torching the White House and Capitol, the British withdrew, and the Foxall

1. Homer L. Calkin, *Castings from the Foundry Mold: A History of Foundry Church, Washington, D.C., 1814–1964* (Nashville: Parthenon Press, 1968).

foundry was spared. True to his word, Foxall gave the money and the new church was built. It was called Foundry to acknowledge the circumstances and also to memorialize an abandoned foundry in London where eighteenth-century Methodists had centered their worship for a period of years.

The original Foundry chapel was erected in 1815. It was renovated, enlarged, and eventually replaced at its first location near the White House. The congregation built the present structure, located approximately one mile north of the White House, on 16th Street in 1904.

Most of my thoughts as I prepared for the new post centered on preaching. I had done a fair amount of preaching through the years, since seminary professors are called on from time to time to do so. But seldom I preached more than once to the same congregation. I didn't use the same sermon everywhere, but truth to tell, I had used some sermons often enough that even I tired of them. I enjoyed preaching. That was one of the main reasons why I accepted the Foundry position. Still, as a busy professor with a host of other administrative and activist involvements, I didn't put a whole lot of time into preparing for the actual delivery of my sermons. I would typically have a full manuscript before me or at least a detailed outline, which of course diminished my eye contact with the congregation. Only God knows whether they were listening intently or sleeping peacefully.

This troubled my conscience. My father had been pastor to a series of small-town churches in Ohio, Arizona, and California. None of these were large churches, but he was an able preacher who took the task seriously. Above all, he prided himself on preaching entirely without notes. When I decided to enter ordained ministry and preached my first sermon in one of his churches in eastern Arizona, he insisted that I also preach without notes. So I did. I continued that practice in my small student church in Marlboro, Massachusetts, during my seminary years. It required more work, but the contact with the listening congregation was obviously better. (The only time I ever went completely blank while preaching was during a preaching practicum at the seminary I was attending. Fortunately, I had a sympathetic teacher who got me through that moment without academic or psychic damage.) Even though I had gotten started in this way, I had drifted away from this approach during my three decades of teaching. Now, as I contemplated Foundry, I resolved to return to the discipline of preaching without manuscript or outline. That spring, as luck would have it, I was due to preach in four or five churches. So I treated this as my "spring training," preparing in each case to preach without notes. It took more time, but I rediscovered the rewards. Having written my first sermon for Foundry, I went into the sanctuary the day before my first Sunday service and preached it—without notes—to the empty sanctuary. This exercise had a further advantage. Attendance would be greatly increased for my second go at this sermon.

I have continued the discipline of preaching without manuscript or outline. The only notes I take with me into the pulpit are quotations I want to read with exactness. I pick these up when the time comes, making it very obvious that I am reading. That has the virtue of making it equally obvious that I am *not* reading when I put the three-by-five card down. Preaching in this way takes more preparation not less, or it could lead to a rambling undisciplined monologue. I almost always write out a complete manuscript for a Sunday sermon, then go through a process of re-outlining, adding new material, sharpening transitions, and struggling to find clearer, simpler ways of saying things without loss of meaning. On my good days, that seems to work out reasonably well. Members of the congregation could probably elaborate on the days that weren't so good—though I continue to marvel at how sometimes when I think I've connected extraordinarily well the response has been unenthusiastic, while at other times when I'm afraid I've bombed, somebody will comment on how helpful the sermon was. We have to do our best, I guess, and leave the results in God's hands.

Having emphasized the advantages of preaching without manuscript, I have to add that some of the greatest preachers I've ever heard have not done it that way. The legendary George Buttrick, for example, was bound to a full manuscript that he shuffled, almost nervously, as he proceeded. But he had great energy, a forceful delivery, and above all, he had something to say that was worth hearing. He had *presence*. So one cannot absolutize method. Still, I believe communication is greatly enhanced by direct eye contact—otherwise, why do political speakers make use of the TelePrompter, which is the best way of pretending that one is speaking without notes? Of course, the first rule of preaching is to have something to say. The late Bishop Gerald Kennedy, himself an extraordinary preacher, used to say that the worst sin for a preacher is not to be interesting. That seemed plausible to me for a time. But then I remembered that history's greatest demagogues have always been interesting. Don't we all wish Adolf Hitler or Joseph McCarthy had been a little *less* captivating? Of course we should strive to be as interesting as possible, but better a dull sermon that is faithful, relevant, and true than an engaging one that is empty or misleading.

The second rule to remember is that the most important sermon is the one that is *heard*, not the one that is written. A preacher quickly learns that a sermon is heard in different ways by different people, depending upon what they bring to it. It will be heard differently by someone who has just lost a loved one, someone who is anxious about possibly losing a job, someone who is facing a major decision, someone who has just gotten engaged, or someone who is present only out of a sense of obligation. The preacher's task is to bear all of the potential audiences in mind, as far as possible. I've never forgotten the church service I attended in New York City in 1961 only hours after hearing of my father's sudden death in far-off California. I don't remember any of the details of the service, only that everybody seemed so insensitive to my overpowering grief. But I hadn't told anybody; how could they have known? So I really couldn't blame anybody for not responding to my loss. From that, I've tried to remember that in a large urban congregation that includes many whom I may not know or know well, there can be people out there who feel the weight of the world on their shoulders.

In going to Foundry I also looked forward to stimulating dialogue with the members of this diverse and well-educated congregation. I would have an opportunity to carry the give-and-take I so loved in the classroom into a broader setting—not just to men and women already committed to the church and ministry but to a host of laypeople involved in exciting pursuits beyond the institutional church. That has in fact happened, sometimes in structured teaching sessions at the church, more often in casual conversation.

People are inhibited from interrupting sermons with questions, which is, on the whole, a blessing. However, I do remember once seeing a hand raised when I was two-thirds of the way through my sermon a year or so after beginning my ministry at Foundry. As a long-time classroom professor, I had a hunch what the raised hand might mean, so I avoided eye contact with the college student, who was likely wanting to ask me a question. I finished the sermon and sat down. Then, before the choir could begin the anthem that was to come next, I heard this voice: "Dr. Wogaman, I have a couple of questions I'd like to ask you." The congregation gasped at the impropriety. But I mounted the pulpit again to hear him out. He wondered about the biblical basis of a controversial portion of my sermon and, furthermore, inquired whether we could include a discussion time as a regular part of the "mass." I recognized him as a Georgetown University undergraduate who had already surfaced in one of our class settings. He was Roman Catholic in background—as reference to our service as a "mass" might suggest—but he had come under the influence of a more fundamentalist group on campus. I responded that we did have numerous opportunities for study and discussion in the church, including specifically the controversial issue that concerned him, but that it would be difficult to provide that opportunity routinely in the much larger and briefer setting of morning worship. We talked a bit more. He sat down, and the service continued. I'll have to admit that I rather enjoyed the exchange and the opportunity to help the congregation see that there are values in the worship setting that transcend decorum. Still, it would be disconcerting to have to deal with such interruptions frequently.

The Bishop Election

The election of new bishops was to occur in July 1992, just three weeks after I began my ministry at Foundry. In the United Methodist Church, such elections are held at a Jurisdictional Conference, one of five geographical bodies of the church in the United States. I was one of those nominated by my own regional body, the Baltimore Conference (now Baltimore-Washington Conference). To say that I had been interested in being elected a bishop would understate the truth, so I had made clear to Bishop Yeakel and the church that if I were elected that would end my tenure at the church. My three-week pastorate would go on record as the shortest in the 180-year history of the church! So we proceeded to Albright College in Pennsylvania, where two new bishops were to be elected.

I entered into the campaigning with enthusiasm. There are proprieties to be observed, of course; one must communicate a sense of being called, but one must not appear too eager nor campaign too aggressively. A dozen or fourteen of us were in the running, each of us given opportunity to speak to the various conference delegations. With appropriate translations, the process and the speeches would be familiar to any student of secular American politics except that, as one wit put it, there may be a whole lot less at stake in church elections than their secular counterparts. We all more or less sincerely wanted to be elected, which means that ten or twelve of us were destined to be disappointed. I was to be among that larger number of nominees.

It has always seemed a bit odd to me that, more often than not, those who are not elected tend to take it quite personally. Maybe this is a consequence of an inflated conception of the position and the honor of being chosen by one's peers for the highest office in the church. Maybe it is an inflated conception of one's own unique abilities, fostered by the enthusiasm of supporters. In any event, it is always the case that many more people are considered than could possibly be elected. Votes *for* one candidate are not usually votes *against* the others. If it is a question of being honored or affirmed, one can say that there is more than enough of that in even being considered. Bishop Yeakel, observing my demeanor during the months prior to this election—and prior to my assuming the Foundry pastorate—remarked to me that being considered for bishop is all right for a Christian, but "don't inhale!"

So it really wasn't so difficult to put that chapter aside. The really interesting thing, psychologically, is that even three weeks at Foundry had been enough to generate a lot of mixed feelings about the bishop prospect. While awaiting results of the first ballot, I mentally visualized that congregation as I had seen it from the pulpit on those first two Sundays. If I were elected bishop I'd have to leave those people. I really liked what I had seen, even in so short a time. After a few ballots it became evident that I wasn't going to be among the elect, so I withdrew and set my sights on Foundry with new enthusiasm.

In retrospect, I believe I wasn't as sensitive as I should have been to the injury that might have been done to this wonderful church by losing a new pastor so soon. It would have taken a while, perhaps a long while, to secure another senior minister. Meanwhile, there could have been a weakening of this downtown congregation.

In that respect, it is worth noting that the United Methodist system rarely uses interim pastors. That appears to violate the conventional wisdom about how a pastorate, especially a long one, needs to be followed by an interim of a year or two while the congregation sorts things out and prepares to move ahead under new leadership. But Foundry's experience does not confirm that judgment. When I assumed my new position in 1992, I was only the fourth senior minister since 1924, and with only one very brief interim along the way. I have noted, in contrast, a number of downtown churches in this and other cities have been damaged by interim arrangements and long search processes. Churches are unique, and what is best for one may not be for others.

Chapter Two

Crisis

In which I have to confront a major crisis while still in the process of getting acquainted with the people of Foundry Church—witness the church's obvious will to survive, despite threatened polarization—receive help from the literature on clergy sexual abuse, but not enough—experience the dilemmas of being an "after-pastor"—work together with church leaders and staff colleagues in the healing—learn about church finance the hard way

Nobody had to tell me that the sermon I would preach on September 20, 1992, could be the most important of my whole ministry. I had been at Foundry only two and a half months when the bombshell hit. The preceding Monday, my predecessor had sent a letter to every member of the congregation expressing regret that he had crossed boundaries in his pastoral relationships with some women in the church. Part of his letter read as follows:

> To put the matter directly, relationships of a sexual nature which I developed with several women in the congregation led to painful and harmful results for them and for me. I want to acknowledge that as the minister it was my responsibility to set the boundaries and to avoid sexual conversation and behavior. I accept responsibility for this violation of my power and my position of authority. I also regret that this injured my ministry as a whole while I was at Foundry.[1]

1. Letter, "To the members of the Foundry Congregation," September 1992.

The letter came as a complete surprise, a shock really, to most of the congregation. A small number had known about the situation. As chairperson of the Conference Board of Ordained Ministry I had been briefed, so far as he was at liberty to do so, by Bishop Yeakel: Several church women had complained to the bishop of inappropriate behavior by the pastor in pastoral settings. They were not suing him, nor filing the kind of formal complaint that might have resulted in a church trial and threatened his loss of clergy credentials, but they considered his behavior serious enough to require attention. The bishop agreed. There proceeded several months of negotiations in which a program of therapy for the pastor was agreed upon. He was due to retire the following June, but in the intervening months he was not to counsel women, his office door was to remain open, and he was not to be in a teaching situation involving women. In late spring several of us, including three lay leaders and Dr. Shropshire, were invited to read the lengthy document to ensure institutional memory. I was included, as senior minister-to-be, although I had not been involved in the negotiations. At no point did I feel bypassed or blindsided in any of this. I was broadly aware of the situation even as I accepted appointment to the church, and I was more relieved than offended not to be included in the negotiations.[2] I would be in a much better position as the new pastor to deal with congregational fallout if I was not directly a part of what had gone before. One could anticipate, accurately as it turned out, that there would be some polarization in the congregation. Without having been an active participant in the negotiations, I might be in a better position to help the church move on.

I did have two or three long conversations with my soon-to-be predecessor. In part, these were to brief me on the overall church situation. But in part they also dealt with Dr. Bauman's sense of remorse over what he had done. I could not condone his pastoral behavior, which had obviously damaged the women in question, including their confidence in the integrity of the church and their own self-regard as persons. None of us knew how much the church as a whole might suffer from this. The women had not wanted their experience to become public, but there was always the chance that it might. It would be exactly the kind of sensational

2. Later, when it became necessary for Dr. Bauman's letter to go out to the congregation, I did enter the discussion of timing. I felt the letter should be mailed out on a Monday so that everybody in the congregation would have time to read it before the following Sunday. I didn't want half the congregation to wonder what was going on when I addressed the issue in my sermon. That request was honored.

story the media seem to thrive on. Through my months of waiting to assume the pastorate I had some anxiety that the story would blow up publicly before I was in a position to deal with it.

At the same time, I had high regard for Dr. Bauman's ministry at Foundry. He had been there twenty-seven-and-a-half years, during which time (and largely as a result of his leadership) the church had become much more progressive, with an increasingly diverse congregation, a vibrant mission outreach program, and a deeper commitment to its ministry. He was, besides, an extraordinarily gifted preacher (once listed by *Time* magazine as one of the top preachers in the nation). His television ministry was widely appreciated across the country. In the spring of 1992 I hoped he would have a positive retirement send-off, that he would receive the kind of personal healing he obviously needed, and above all that those who had been injured by his pastoral abuses would find the healing they needed. And I hoped that it would all be resolved without disrupting the church I was about to serve. I looked forward to being able to invite him back to preach again, and told him so.

In hindsight, the situation had to become public, and perhaps it is best that it should have. Too often there is a tendency to sweep such things under the rug. The result is that situations are never really healed and, sometimes, that serious misbehavior can continue unchecked. There can be a kind of vague unease in a community, even a church, that people don't quite understand. It can be better to let things become public if they can then be dealt with in a responsible way. I wouldn't have put it that way during those months of preparation for leadership at Foundry, but my anxieties were influencing me too much.[3]

As it turned out, I had two and a half months as senior minister before the story broke with the sending of Dr. Bauman's letter. What precipitated the letter was the complainants' discovery that they were not the only people in the church who had been hurt. They felt they had been misled; more than that, they felt that there might be still more women in the church who needed to be ministered to. They insisted that Dr. Bauman himself write the congregation. This brought on a new series of negotiations that

3. Subsequent attention to the growing literature on this subject was helpful to many of us. That included such books as Marie M. Fortune, *Is Nothing Sacred? When Sex Invades the Pastoral Relationship* (San Francisco: HarperSanFrancisco, 1992); Peter Rutter, M.D., *Sex in the Forbidden Zone: When Men in Power—Therapists, Doctors, Clergy, Teachers, and Others—Betray Women's Trust* (New York: Ballantine Books, 1989); and Karen Lebacqz and Ronald G. Barton, *Sex in the Parish* (Louisville, Ky.: Westminster/John Knox Press, 1991).

occurred during my first weeks at Foundry, and then the letter went out to the whole congregation.

I give Bishop Yeakel credit for his clearheaded handling of all this. He arranged to meet the church's Administrative Board after the letter was in the mail but not yet received. Most of the nearly one hundred board members present were of course shocked. He answered their questions patiently, and allowed them to vent their feelings. Looking over the transcript of that discussion now, ten years later, I am impressed by his leadership and by the generally civil tone of the participants. At the time, the atmosphere was electric with emotion. Some defended their former pastor, feeling he had been dealt with too harshly, that maybe he had been railroaded in some way. Others voiced their disappointment, even disillusionment. Other churches, facing similar situations, have often become polarized between defenders and critics. Evidence of polarization among Foundry's leaders was clear in the two or three hours of discussion that night. Still, some of the wise old heads of the church had a calming effect. At the end, I was invited to draw things together. I'm not sure I did that very well. I do remember being impressed at the time that the Foundry people had a strong will to survive as a vibrant church despite deep differences over the matter at hand. The board decided that the Informal Coordinating Committee—a kind of unofficial executive committee comprised of a handful of church leaders—should develop a strategy for the church's response.

That night was also my introduction to press relations. After the meeting concluded, I found our minister of administration, Rev. Paul Vali, in the church's reception booth, his hand cupped over the telephone. A reporter from the *Washington Post* was on the line, he announced, wanting my comments on what had been revealed in the meeting. How could they have known so quickly! Sooner or later I would have to respond to the reporter. But realizing that the *Post* could hardly run the story in the next morning's edition without a comment from me, I elected to dodge the call for the time being. I wanted as many people as possible in the church to receive the letter before they read about it in the newspaper; besides, the Informal Coordinating Committee was to meet early the next morning, and I needed their counsel.

The committee decided, wisely, that the church should not try to hide anything, so later I did speak to the *Post* and also to a young reporter, fresh out of journalism school, at the much more conservative *Washington Times*. The committee began to work on long-range strategy in cooperation with the church's Committee on the Status and Role of Women.

There would be structured opportunities for people to work through their feelings. The women who had been abused in this pastoral relationship would be given opportunities for therapy at the church's expense—not only those who had gone to the bishop but any others who might surface. Women on the church's ministerial staff would be especially open to helping women in the church.

The Service

Then there was the question of the service the following Sunday. It was agreed that I should speak candidly with the congregation during the "concerns" period, the time in the service when parish announcements and other concerns are dealt with more informally. By Sunday, most of the people would have gotten their copies of the letter and probably also read about it in their newspapers.

I knew that my sermon would be an especially important opportunity to interpret the situation in the light of our shared faith, but I also knew that my previously announced topic would no longer do. As I awakened early in the morning after the Administrative Board meeting, the words of a member, Martha Brooke, were ringing in my ears. Martha had said at the meeting, "Only truth heals." Yes of course, I thought, my sermon title will be "Truth Heals." I would develop it around the different layers of truth we have to sort through: the truth about the hurt experienced by the women and that we must not allow this to happen again, the truth that Dr. Bauman's ministry had really contributed extraordinary gifts to the congregation and many of its members and that one did not have to repudiate any of that; above all, that the truth we proclaim is expressed in Jesus Christ, in whose spirit all these things can be worked through.

It was no surprise that attendance that Sunday was very high! Somehow we got through it all. People had been shaken by the letter and the newspaper coverage. I proceeded as planned with the "truth heals" theme. I acknowledged that I had known about the misbehavior when I first preached at Foundry two and a half months earlier, and that I had, nevertheless, meant the positive things I had said then about Dr. Bauman's ministry at Foundry. That was an important part of the truth. At the same time, I acknowledged that the abuses of pastoral privilege had really hurt people and that that kind of behavior must stop, whether it is in the church or in the secular settings where most of Foundry's people work. Congregational response was positive but muted. People were still hurting. Some were outraged by what they had learned. Some were critical of the whistle-blowers, feeling that a beloved pastor had been falsely maligned. Some were disillusioned, having based much of their faith upon this man. Some worried about the future of the church. Some were, I suppose, just confused by it all. But despite the differences of reaction, the church hadn't blown apart. My instincts told me we would be able to weather the storm.

As luck would have it, my installation service had been planned for that very afternoon. (Actually, in the United Methodist Church it is more a service of recognition and celebration, since one is "installed" on arrival.) Several people made nice speeches, and I affirmed a set of vows that had been written for the occasion. Nothing was said about the crisis that had engulfed the church, but it seemed to help all of us to reaffirm the church and look ahead. It certainly helped me. The vows themselves helped to focus my mind beyond the present crisis, and since they represented my aspirations for the coming years, they should be recorded here. Each of the questions was put by Gary Allen, the church's lay leader. My response to the first was "I do." To each of the rest the response was "I will, God being my helper."

> Philip, do you, in the presence of this congregation, reaffirm your ordination vows and willingly and joyfully commit yourself to this position of trust and responsibility?
>
> Will you be among us as one whose life is grounded in Christian faith? Will you seek to be led by God in all things?
>
> Will you be among us as a caring and trusted pastor? Will you love the members of this congregation, seeking always what is best for them as persons and what is best for this church as a community of faith?
>
> Will you preach the word of God, as it is given to you, winsomely and fearlessly? Will you endeavor to be both prophet and priest? Will you respect the views of others who, in good faith, disagree with you?
>
> Will you be among us as an advocate for social justice? Will you be a spokesperson for God's will in this city and nation, especially as a voice for those of God's beloved who have no voice?
>
> Will you ground your ministry among us in disciplined study and prayer?

A concluding, very down-to-earth question was, "Will you take time for relaxation and restoration, and for your own family and loved ones?"

Ten years later, I still think those are very good questions! They are exactly the right questions. The answer is also exactly the right answer:

"I will, God being my helper." But the performance? Ah, that is another matter! Insofar as my performance fell short of these noble aspirations, we cannot blame God for being an inadequate helper.

Having pondered these vows and having been fortified in the service by words of congratulation and challenge (felicitously stretching the truth about my capabilities), it was time to get to work. And the task at hand remained helping the congregation through the crisis none of us had wanted.

Moving Ahead

Since most of the literature on clergy sexual misconduct tends to neglect the question of how a church should cope with such a crisis, we had to play it by ear. My sermon was but a first step. The decision by church leaders to be truthful with the press was another, and an important one. That communicated to the wider world that Foundry had nothing to hide and that the church was confident about its own future—a message the congregation also needed to see reinforced in the public media.

At the more direct level, church leaders decided to offer special opportunities for counsel and just talking it out. Offered each Sunday following the second service, the sessions were separated by gender—which meant that I would not personally participate in the meetings of women. The meetings continued for several weeks. Attendance was fairly small, but we continued to remind people about the sessions regularly, and I believe most people received this as evidence of the church's responsiveness even if they did not participate. During this period we also announced that any women who had personally been hurt by boundary-crossing violations could be provided with professional therapy at the church's expense. To my knowledge, no one accepted this offer, but I'm sure it helped everybody to know that the church cared enough to respond in this way. The counseling opportunities, both on a group and an individual basis, continued to be announced publicly for two or three months.

During the same period, Carolyn and I spent two or three evenings per week in get-acquainted sessions with people in the church. These had not been arranged with an eye toward any particular problems or crises but simply to give us a chance to meet people in the church and for them to meet us. All were held in homes, with seven evenings in the District of Columbia, seven in Virginia suburbs, and seven in nearby Maryland. Attendance varied from a dozen or so people to thirty or forty. Only one of these evening meetings had happened before the crisis hit the church, so the remaining twenty of the sessions were in fact available to help people process things further. I invited people to say whatever they wanted and ask any questions they wanted. I tried to phrase this in such a way that people would feel free to deal with the problem that was on everybody's mind but not feel obligated to raise the issue. It became a central topic in about two-thirds of the conversations. Sometimes a parishioner would catch me privately before or after the meeting time for an observation or question.

The reactions and questions were wide ranging, but I don't recall any real conflict breaking out. Some parishioners were vocally critical of the former pastor, and some felt his accusers had gone too far. The conversations were serious and civil and by no means limited to the crisis, and when we completed the series we felt we knew the church much better. We had dramatically increased the circle of immediate acquaintance. We had a better feel for the church's extended geographical sweep in the District, Maryland, and Virginia. Every Sunday, we could now see, our congregation gathered from many places. The neighborhood gatherings helped us picture the kinds of settings people were coming from—and not incidentally their different mind-sets on a range of subjects. We could see the great diversity of the church more clearly. But it was also clear to us that Foundry was made up of people who valued one another and their church very much. Much of the credit for that certainly belonged to the one whose pastoral misbehavior had also brought anguish.

I continued to deal with that anguish more directly as a pastor in subsequent months and even years. Sometimes people came to my office seeking spiritual counsel, sometimes we would have a meaningful private exchange before or after some meeting or in another more accidental setting. The most poignant of these involved people who had obviously built their spiritual lives around the influence of the former pastor and were now disillusioned. I recall one couple who spoke of significant economic and professional decisions they had made on the basis of his influence, and now their spiritual assurance had collapsed. What could I say? I had to find words to convey that insofar as he had led them to deeper levels of commitment, even to very sacrificial commitment, they could still affirm that. I suppose such thoughts could only be half believed. All of this came as a stark reminder of how much we base our spiritual lives upon the models provided by others. True, all of us are sinners, and no spiritual model or mentor is without flaws. Still, when a charismatic preacher is shown to have clay feet like everybody else—if not worse—the aftermath of disillusionment can be especially great. Possibly every spiritual disillusionment is also an invitation to abandon unrealistic illusions. Illusions about leaders tend to increase in proportion to their charisma.

In recent years the Catholic Church has had to confront the problem in a different way. While most Catholic priests are not noted for their charismatic preaching, they do embody an aura of sanctity flowing from their sacramental office. For many laypersons in the Catholic tradition, the priest's powers are a divine gift. Therefore, when a priest "falls" (as in the pedophilia cases), the whole sacramental tradition can be called into question. Never mind that Roman Catholic theology carefully distinguishes between the ultimate validity of the sacrament and the character of the priest who administers it. For the lay mind this is a very difficult distinction to make when the priest, as representative of Christ, is obviously un-Christlike.

The problem is compounded when, as sometimes happens in a Protestant setting, an especially compelling preacher embodies, to the layperson, the very faith itself. When the preacher "falls," so may the faith of the person whose whole spiritual life has been shaped and modeled under his or her influence. The highly publicized scandals involving televangelists Jim Bakker and Jimmy Swaggart had that effect. In my opinion, Dr. Bauman's ministry had a good deal more substance than that of those figures, and his pastoral violations seemed less egregious. Nevertheless, several Foundry people were put through a spiritual crisis. The pastoral problem was to help these people see that a good deal of his message was true and good, even if he, as messenger, had fallen short.

We were facing the same question that had been raised long ago. Is the faith of the church and the spiritual helpfulness of its worship and sacraments dependent upon the character of the clergy? That issue was settled in Catholic theology in Augustine's controversy with the Donatists, who argued that the character of the priest establishes the validity of Baptism, Eucharist, and other sacraments. Augustine's view was that the sacraments are from Christ, who alone confers validity upon them. The priest, be his character good, bad, or indifferent, is merely the channel of what comes from Christ. That answer, good as far as it goes, may not say enough. Clearly it helps when we have before us human examples of how the gospel can be put into practice. Yet if clergy are inevitably flawed to some degree, that does not mean that the faith itself must be abandoned.

The Awkwardness of Being an "After-Pastor"

In one of our talk-back sessions, a young man observed that one problem was that too many people had put the preacher on a pedestal. He had become the center of focus, sometimes the object of adoration, whether or not that was his intention. Naturally that had set the church up for disillusionment when his practice didn't measure up to his message. I thought that was a valid point. A test of great preaching is always whether it can direct the gaze of the people away from the preacher and bring it to rest on the living God. The better the preacher is, the more difficult that can be!

So the young man's point was well taken. But I had to face the fact that it wasn't just about Dr. Bauman; it was also about me! I don't think I occupied a pedestal in quite the same way, and yet the pulpit I did occupy was exactly the same one he had preached from. How was I to be perceived by the congregation, standing where he stood? In the literature on clergy misbehavior there is occasional mention of the "after-pastor," the pastor who comes after and has to deal with the consequences. That is what I was, an "after-pastor." I was learning that one of those consequences is that one must bear a weight of suspicion. It is as though there were people saying, "All right, Phil, now what are you going to be like?" One of my clergy friends remarked that when a colleague in ministry violates pastoral trust it makes it twice as difficult for the rest of us, for all of us then have to bear some additional burden of mistrust.[4] In retrospect, ten years later, I think that wasn't as much a reality as I feared at the time. Yet the fear was real enough.

How was I to deal with it? In part by being scrupulously careful about any actions or talk that could be misconstrued. Many pastors, myself included, find it easy and natural to hug somebody of either gender in an expression of caring that has nothing to do with sex. But for a time I had to limit that kind of gesture. I've generally followed the practice of keeping the office door open, or at least ajar, when counseling or conferring with women—a practice the Rev. Billy Graham has adhered to throughout his long ministry. As an after-pastor I could see the point of that more clearly.

There was another, more subtle problem, arriving from the opposite direction. A number of people in the church continued to feel that the events had been taken out of proportion and that the former minister was himself being misused. Whenever I spoke about the issue, it could be understood by some as an effort to make myself look good by making him look bad! I really didn't think of our relationship in competitive terms, but that is what some might have thought. I'm not at all sure that anybody did

4. In a similar vein, Marie Fortune remarks, "Most pastors maintain the sacred trust bestowed upon them when they are ordained. But some do not. And those who do not, few though they may be, seriously diminish the credibility of the majority who do" (Fortune, *Is Nothing Sacred?* 130).

perceive me in that way, but that did not keep me from worrying about it. So there was another source of awkwardness.

Perhaps I've overstated the problems of an after-pastor. They are real enough, but they are not as serious as I felt they were at the time. Time, in fact, is what is finally most helpful. Time and patience. Whatever problems of mistrust one might confront are best dealt with in the most obvious way: by building trust through faithful pastoral service. At some point (I couldn't tell you exactly when), those after-pastor problems just didn't seem to be there anymore. In Foundry's case there was another factor at work: A whole lot of our people had themselves been through personal difficulties of one kind or another. Having found a degree of healing in the church for themselves, they were better able to put the crisis in perspective. Even in their disagreements with one another over this or other issues, Foundry's people have a remarkably open spirit.

Discovering a Shared Ministry

Carolyn was especially helpful through this whole period. Sharing fully in the neighborhood meetings and other settings, her processing of what we were experiencing together helped me perceive things I simply wouldn't have gotten otherwise. I came to rely on her pastoral perceptions very much throughout our time together at Foundry. The fact that we had both arrived at this form of pastoral ministry so late in life meant that she was neither captured by nor threatened by earlier Protestant conceptions of a minister's wife's role. She could be her own mature self. The traditional role of the minister's spouse was already disappearing in 1992, with increased numbers of women in the pulpit, more unmarried clergy, and an almost universal pattern of working spouses of married clergy. Carolyn had recently retired, but the Foundry congregation never sought to fit her into any kind of mold. She was free to continue volunteer work outside the church, and within the church to be a part of whatever activities and ministries she was attracted to. Through that first pastoral crisis and for the next ten years, I found her perceptions and counsel to be invaluable.

In those early months, I also grew to respect and appreciate the church staff more and more. I had inherited all of them except my own secretary, Susan Bender—who, in addition to being an unusually competent assistant, was also Foundry's soprano soloist. Dr. Walter Shropshire, who was designated as "minister of the parish," was probably my closest collaborator and confidant. Walt had been a leading biophysicist at the Smithsonian Institution in Washington before getting his seminary degree and entering full-time pastoral ministry as a second career. Coincidentally, he had taken a couple of classes of mine at Wesley Seminary a few years earlier, completing them with distinction. He had come to Foundry one year before me and helped me get my feet on the ground. He had been fully apprised of the impending crisis months before it broke. Together we gave the rest of the staff a "heads up" before most of the rest of the congregation got the news, so that we could all engage in the pastoral challenge together.

I had also known Dr. Eileen Guenther, the minister of music and worship, at Wesley Seminary, where she was organist, choral director, and adjunct professor of church music. Eileen was known throughout the Washington area as one of the real leaders in church music. She and I were to have a very close working relationship in preparations for worship services.

Betty Dunlop had joined the church staff a few months earlier as minister of Christian education. On my first day at the church she greeted me with, "God sent you here so we could all have computers." I had in fact noted to the trustees that computers had become a virtual necessity. She gave staff leadership to organizing the neighborhood meetings along with prime responsibility for the church's various educational programs.

Rev. Paul Vali, the minister of administration, had formal responsibility for fiscal management, supervision of support staff, and building management. Informally, he was the in-house humorist, with witty comments to lighten any difficult situation. Harry Engin rounded out the professional staff as minister of missions. Harry was a retired communications executive. He was strongly committed to hands-on forms of mission activity, such as the development of a Friday morning time for homeless people to be received at the church for counsel, referrals, clothing, and other services.

The six of us were called "equipping ministers," a 1970s designation embodying the idea that professional clergy are there to equip the laity for their various forms of ministry. The staff also included several persons in secretarial roles, a number of them part-time. Altogether it was quite a crew.[5] Each of my colleagues had an assigned set of responsibilities, but the job descriptions were flexible enough that each could share in the work of others as needed. I had a nice illustration of that on my second Sunday

5. Over the ten years Carolyn and I were at Foundry, almost all of the support staff positions changed. But the only "equipping ministry" positions to change throughout those years were the minister of missions and minister of Christian education.

at Foundry. I had just completed the parish announcements and concerns, and I was then to announce the passing of the peace—a time when the gathered congregants would greet one another. But I forgot and returned to my chair behind the pulpit. Without missing a beat, Walt stepped forward to say the traditional words, "As a forgiven people let us now exchange signs of peace and reconciliation." Ouch, I thought. I was supposed to do that! I went out into the congregation to greet people and then headed back into the chancel area to resume my place. As I passed Walt, and before I could thank him, he said, "You're welcome."

Our sharing of responsibilities through the years often took place at more serious levels. That included pastoral care for people in distress, participation in educational programs, supporting the mission ventures, helping with worship services. I quickly learned that even though I was senior minister I must be prepared to deal with a wide range of tasks. My role meant that while I didn't have primary responsibility for the areas covered by my colleagues, I had to be ready to back them up and to offer suggestions.

Our ability to function as a team was tested to the limit when the crisis of September 1992 struck the church. We had specialized tasks: For instance, Betty Dunlop helped arrange the sessions for women desiring counsel and opportunity to express their feelings, and I was the church's spokesperson with the press. Betty and Eileen, as the women on our team, made themselves available to offer pastoral counsel to women who felt uncomfortable with the rest of us, as men, during this time. But all of us tried to stay alert to emerging problems and to consult with one another frequently. We were drawn together through this experience. I think all of us came to a much deeper sense of the church as a community of faith under the grace of God.

It is said that a church never really recovers from this kind of crisis, but I do not agree. Major events in the life of institutions, as of individuals and families, become defining moments. But they can bring out the best in us. They do not have to become a kind of unchangeable karma that determines our future. We can learn from things and then move on.

I had hoped to be able to invite Dr. Bauman back to preach sometime, thus fulfilling an implied commitment dating from our first conversations. For a long time that would have been too polarizing or at least too likely to open up old wounds. At two or three points along the way I was prepared to issue the invitation, but then something would come up to make me pause again. But if a church is to be a reconciling community, it cannot be unforgiving. Dr. Bauman had made major contributions to the development of this church as such a community. His return to the pulpit could, I believed, bring healing. The time seemed fitting, I thought, during my last summer at Foundry, in 2002. By then there were hundreds of new people in the congregation; his preaching could help them have a better historical sense of the church. For others, regardless of how they had experienced the initial trauma, it could be a moment of grace.

I discussed the possibility with our Staff-Parish Relations Committee and with the staff itself, working through the initial skepticism of some. Over lunch I broached the possibility with Ed himself. After voicing some concerns, he thanked me and we agreed on a date. My advice to him was that he touch only briefly on the past but then bring his own fresh message to the people. He did, and in my judgment the net effect of his coming was very positive. It did not mean that his flawed pastoral behavior hadn't mattered, but that it is possible to move on and that in the end we are not defined by our sins and imperfections.

Learning about Church Finances—the Hard Way

As a matter of fact, even that early part of my pastoral journey was not defined entirely by the crisis. Some very positive things were happening, but I was also learning some important things about church administration, things they didn't teach us about in seminary (I can't believe I really said that!). Mainly I was learning that, while the church is not about money, it can't run without enough of it.

My learning curve began with two visits to my office. The first was by Kirk Griffith, chair of the Finance Committee, which had the responsibility of finalizing the church budget for the coming year. He had come in to ask whether I thought we should scale the budget back substantially in light of the pastoral transition and, perhaps, also in light of what had been happening in the church. He raised the question tactfully. He didn't directly voice whatever doubts he may have had about my ability to maintain the level of support the church had enjoyed previously. In fact, I may have had more doubts about that than he did, but it also seemed to me that to downscale the budget now would send exactly the wrong message. Let's just assume the support will be there, I said. If it isn't, we can adjust to that later. But let's convey a sense of optimism and forward movement. He agreed with that and, in fact, the pledge campaign didn't do all that badly. But I was reminded that the material support of a large congregation is not simply to be taken for granted. As a seminary professor, and even as the dean of the faculty, I had not had to bear such responsibility for the fiscal well-being of the whole institution. Now I could not avoid it.

That point was underscored by the second visit, this time from Genevieve Taylor, the longtime church treasurer. Genevieve's commitments to the church ran deep. Then in her eighties, she had been a part of the generation of young women who migrated to Washington, D.C., at the outset of World War II and never left. She served in positions of increasing responsibility in the Department of Defense prior to her retirement a few years before I came to Foundry. She had been a member of the church for decades. Genevieve had come to my office to give me a lesson or two about church finance. She showed me the figures. A church like Foundry, located in the downtown of a great city and with more than two thousand people in its membership and wider constituency, needs to have a reserve cushion equal to at least three months of expenses. But the operating surplus had dipped to around sixty to seventy thousand dollars. That seemed like a lot of money to my untrained eye, but it was less than one month's expenses. Alarmingly, the surplus had been declining for several years, which meant we were living beyond our means. Either we'd have to increase income or decrease expenses; the moment of truth was approaching.

Eileen stopped by the office on other business, and I confided in her that I was beginning to get worried about the budget. Please worry! she said. Somebody around here needs to worry! I don't know that I was really worried, for there were too many other signs of health in the church, and we did always have the option of scaling back. But Kirk and Genevieve had gotten my attention. I simply *had* to pay attention to church finances and do what I could to (1) increase levels of support and (2) ensure that the church was spending its money wisely—that we should, in theological terms, be good stewards.

Things got better over time. But I had learned to keep a watchful eye. I had learned that, no matter how large or affluent a church, there can be deficits at any level. I learned as well that there is a deep correlation between a congregation's commitment to its basic mission and its sacrificial giving. Over the years, as the congregation responded with great generosity to specific needs, such as the relief of a sister church damaged by the Oklahoma City bombing and assistance to refugees in Kosovo, I have also learned that generous giving in one area is not necessarily in competition with giving for other needs and the ongoing program of the church. Generosity can be habit forming.

The Crisis Eases

I cannot say exactly when the mood of crisis ended. Through the last months of 1992 we had done a number of things to address it. The neighborhood dessert and conversation evenings had helped, as had the multiple efforts by my colleagues and the church's lay leadership. Toward the end of the year I could detect a mounting impatience with the frequent announcements about the dialogue and counseling opportunities and other references to the process of healing. People move at different rates of speed; clearly many were now ready to move on. Meanwhile I had not often addressed the subject directly in my sermons. That was partly because I had other things I wanted to speak about—for instance, that fall included the 500th anniversary of Columbus's "discovery" of America as well as a presidential election, and I had also wanted to give the congregation a better sense of what the overall preaching agenda would be in the days and years ahead.

Nevertheless, it was getting close to the time for a major sermonic effort on forgiveness and the healing of wounded relationships. My approach would be very direct, and I felt the congregation was about ready for that. In my preaching schedule ahead, I planned to do that on Sunday, March 14, 1993. But something happened that weekend to change my plans and to alter the course of Foundry's future in ways none of us could have predicted.

Chapter Three

Guess Who's Coming to Church

In which we are advised by weather forecasters to cancel services, but stay open anyway—serve the homeless and are surprised by unexpected visitors—cope with new security problems and face new dilemmas in preaching—help the congregation adjust to extraordinary challenges and opportunities—try not to take ourselves too seriously

The weekend of March 13–14, 1993, was one of the coldest, snowiest, and windiest we had ever seen in Washington. The whole Northeast was bitterly cold. Records were being set in many cities. The snow began Friday evening and continued all day Saturday. By mid-afternoon I was wondering about the sermon I had planned for the next day.

It was going to be that sermon on forgiveness. I had hoped with it to bring more closure to the congregation's conflicted feelings over the past few months. The sermon would explore the central importance of forgiveness in Christian life, while acknowledging the difficulty of forgiving when you have really been hurt or betrayed. This can be an exquisitely complicated subject, which is why I hadn't tried to deal with it so directly in the first months of Foundry's crisis. Now, in mid-March, I thought we were ready to think together about what it means to forgive, really forgive, and move on. But, of course, that couldn't happen if most of the congregation wasn't able to get to church!

I called my friend and former pastor Bill Holmes to see what he was planning to do at Metropolitan Memorial United Methodist Church. He had already decided to go ahead with his Sunday service but to merge the usual two services into one, to keep it informal, and to shelve his announced sermon. That made sense to me, although I thought it wise to keep to our usual schedule of 9:30 and 11:00 services. I would postpone the forgiveness sermon to a later date and come up with something else for tomorrow. What might that be? My inspiration of the moment was to take the bitter storm itself as a kind of metaphor, asking what we are to do when life dumps things on us and there isn't anything we can do about it. The famous serenity prayer came to mind: "Lord, grant me the serenity to accept the things I cannot change, the courage to change the things I can, and the wisdom to know the difference." Various illustrative stories, some from my own experience, fell easily into place. This could be kept informal, and it would certainly be relevant to what everybody was actually experiencing.

That night, as the snow passed the twelve-inch level and kept accumulating, Carolyn and I watched the TV news. A weather forecaster announced that, with bitter cold and brisk winds, the windchill was now well below zero. He then said that he was going to give some advice he never thought he would have to: "Please," he said, "don't try to go to church tomorrow."

Did that translate into advice to pastors to cancel their services? In fact, many pastors in the region did exactly that: Probably over half of the churches of the metropolitan area were closed. What should we do? With a congregation spread out in all directions, it seemed clear to Carolyn and me that there was no way we could communicate with everybody, which meant that some people were bound to show up even if we did cancel. And if some people could make it, why couldn't we? Fortunately for us, we live only half a mile from a Metro subway station. We could get off at the Dupont Circle station, just half a mile from the church at the other end. We made our way up Brandywine Street, through the snowdrifts, with biting winds at our backs. The subway trains were running just fine, so we got to church. One member of the custodial staff also made it and began clearing pathways to the doors. My secretary, Susan Bender, and her husband were also able to get to church, as was Greg Calpaldini, the 9:30 service music coordinator. Everybody else on the church staff was snowed in. Susan busied herself with putting food together in brown paper bags for a number of homeless people who came to the door, later arranging musical alternatives for the second service with telephoned advice from the snowbound Eileen. Carolyn took over the phone system, responding to numerous calls from people wondering whether services would be held. I moved the 9:30 service from the main sanctuary to the smaller chapel. Perhaps two dozen people arrived for that. We had a beautiful Communion together, and I presented my "What do you do when life dumps on you?" sermon. While Greg was playing a postlude on the chapel piano, I went to the rear door to greet the small congregation as they left.

Carolyn met me at the door. "Guess who's coming to church," she smiled. I was surprised that *anybody* was coming to church! "Somebody is here from the Secret Service, and President and Mrs. Clinton are *walking* up from the White House for the 11:00 service." On impulse, I turned back to the 9:30 congregation to relay this news. They might want to stay for the second service.

There really wasn't time to get nervous. Homeless people needed assistance, the music arrangements had to be pulled together, somebody had to figure out how to work the P.A. system in the sanctuary. We never did solve the P.A. problem. I was still too new to the church to know how to set that up, and nobody else seemed to know anything about it. Fortunately, Foundry has excellent acoustics, even in the large sanctuary, so we got by. Some twenty choir members made it, and between Susan and Greg that turned out quite well. Linda Brubaker played and sang "Amazing Grace" with her autoharp. Everything fell into place.

Before the service began, I was alerted to the approach of the president and first lady, a gaggle of press people, and an indeterminate number of Secret Service agents, enough of them, all told, to about double the congregation. Having walked the mile from the White House in the bitter wind, the procession looked a bit bedraggled as they approached the door. Hillary walked in first, holding out her hand and giving us a cheery greeting. Then in came the president of the United States, ruddy of face and cheerful of smile. I welcomed them both and then escorted the procession down the hallway to the sanctuary. The service began.

This was the first time I had ever met a president, and I still wonder why I wasn't more nervous. Perhaps it was that it had all happened so quickly. Perhaps it was that President Clinton is considerably younger than I. Perhaps it was just that they were both very friendly. And maybe it was the larger challenge of the weather. The choir, with Susan as impromptu director, did beautifully—evidence of its years of coaching by Eileen. Greg performed well, even though, as he confessed later, he was almost beside himself with nervousness. Having already had one run-through, the sermon helped keep me steady, although I did make one modest change. While continuing to emphasize the "serenity to accept the things I cannot change" theme, I added some lines on the "courage to change the things I can" portion of the classic prayer. After all, I thought, the president of the United States *can* change a whole lot of things, and I don't want him to be too "serene" about the needs and injustices of a broken world that he is in a position to do something about.

After the service, the Clintons lingered to greet everybody. The atmosphere was warm and friendly, like a small church "down home" somewhere, I thought. Foundry Church practices such hospitality all the time, despite its size. But facing adversity together often contributes to the bonding of people, and so it was with all of us that day.

The Clintons Become Regulars

While the Clintons' attendance at Foundry on March 14 was a complete surprise, we had rather expected them to show up some Sunday. Along with a number of downtown pastors, I had written a welcoming letter shortly after the election in November. (A year or so later, I learned that that letter had gotten lost among the thousands of letters received at then-Governor Clinton's Little Rock address.) Since President Clinton was a Baptist and his wife and daughter were United Methodists, press speculation had centered around various Washington Baptist churches for him and two or three United Methodist churches, including Foundry, for Hillary and Chelsea. Quite apart from my letter, I knew that a number of mutual acquaintances from Arkansas had commended Foundry to them—and, of course, the church is located on 16th Street, only a mile north of the White House.

In fact, Foundry people were excited enough about the prospect of their coming to our church that I felt compelled on the Sunday after the inauguration to preach on "reflected glory," with the 2 Corinthians 4:6 text about the glory of God reflected in the face of Jesus Christ. That is the only "reflected glory" that should concern us much. I kidded the congregation a bit about the Washington tendency to bask in the reflected glory of people and institutions of great power and prestige, and I quoted from a *Washington Post* account of an elderly African American preacher, many of whose flock had deserted his church to attend a neighboring church where the president-elect and vice-president-elect were to be present. The wise old preacher understood the human motivations at work on historic occasions and was not critical of his members, but, he reminded them, the Holy Spirit is always present in our church! That was, I thought, the right attitude. But, along with many of our congregation, I'm not sure I always attained that level of Christian maturity myself!

The Clintons came next on May 9, and after that with increasing frequency. By the next fall and winter they had become regulars. Throughout the remainder of the president's eight years in office they attended somewhat more than once a month—rather remarkable in light of his schedule of travel and other obligations. All three members of the family retained their formal membership in their Little Rock churches—he at the Immanuel Baptist Church, Hillary and Chelsea at First United Methodist—but after a few months they began to worship together at Foundry.

Since May 9 was only their second time at Foundry, we did not yet know what to expect. I still chuckle over what happened during the passing of the peace in that service. The youth choir had just sung. During the passing of the peace, the worshipers are encouraged to greet their neighbors with traditional words of peace and reconciliation. It is a beautiful custom, and especially beautiful at Foundry where there is real warmth in the greetings. As I might have anticipated but did not, a line formed in the vicinity of the president and first lady. What an opportunity to greet and shake hands with a president! I could have brought that to an end at any point, but I noticed the robed figures of the youth choir all lined up, each awaiting a turn to meet the president. This, I thought, might be the only opportunity these young people ever have for such a thing, so I let it continue until the last of the youth had passed the peace with the president and gone back to their appointed places. After the service, one of the young people held up her hand, announcing that she had actually shaken hands with the president of the United States and would never wash her hand again! In later weeks, after presidential visits had become more regular, the invitation to pass the peace was amended to include the words "with your nearest neighbors."

Extraordinary Measures to Preserve the Ordinary

Occasionally I am asked whether the presence of a president requires any special arrangements. The short answer is yes, of course! But those special arrangements are not designed to magnify the importance of the president's attendance. Exactly the opposite: They are needed to allow things to proceed as normally as possible. That takes some doing.

The first few Sundays, before visits by the first family could be predicted, security arrangements were a bit lighter. Secret Service agents were on hand from the beginning, but it was not necessary to put people through metal detectors. Visitors were "magged" with hand-held detectors, and regular attendees who were identified by our staff were let through without even that much examination. After a few weeks, however, when presidential visits were more predictable, the Secret Service examined the church with great care and set up metal detectors that were not unlike those in airports. Having to go through metal detectors took some getting used to. Most people accepted the necessity and adjusted gracefully, but we still laugh about one visitor who had just moved to town. Seeing the big stone church down 16th Street from her new home, she decided to check it out the next Sunday. But, as she later reported, she was surprised to see police cars just outside the main church doors. What could that mean? Then, proceeding through the door into the narthex, she encountered metal detectors. As she later reported in a membership class, that took her completely by surprise. She had heard that the District of Columbia had a crime problem, but was it so bad that the churches had to have metal detectors?

On the whole, the Secret Service impressed us as very thorough, very professional, and very courteous. They bent over backward to keep from disrupting things. Walt Shropshire and Paul Vali worked most closely with them, occasionally asking them to adjust some procedure to make things go more smoothly for the congregation. For instance, they agreed to establish more metal detector units so people wouldn't have to stand in line quite so long, and they helped cut noise levels down in the narthex so as not to disturb our services. A command unit was established in one of the church rooms, with direct phone communication. At one point they asked whether we would be willing to refrain from ringing our church bells so agents could be posted in the bell tower. We have six magnificent bells, ringing in melodic cadence at the beginning and end of each service. That has become such an important part of our tradition—sending a much appreciated message of spiritual presence for blocks around—that we were reluctant to bend on that point. So the Secret Service made other arrangements. I'm sure I still don't know what all of their arrangements to protect the first family were. I was impressed by the number of agents and the thoroughness of their work. At the Secret Service's request, I usually escorted the Clintons out of the church immediately following the benediction, before the rest of the congregation exited. That was partly to ensure that the president wouldn't be trapped by well-wishers and autograph seekers, and partly, I suppose, on the theory that the senior minister could help keep things orderly. So, just before the benediction, I would say something like, "The congregation is requested to remain in place for a few moments following the benediction." Everybody knew what that meant, and overall we had almost no incidents before, during, or after services.

The fact that we had almost no incidents through nearly eight years speaks volumes about the effectiveness of the Secret Service and our own staff people, ushers, and greeters. The one incident we all do remember occurred during the second service on Easter Sunday, April 3, 1994. The early part of the service that Easter had proceeded normally, which, for Easter, also means joyously. The overflow congregation was in a great mood, and the choir was in its usual fine form, accompanied by organ and trumpets. My sermon was to be on "Profound Joy," not the more superficial joyousness of the Palm Sunday entry into Jerusalem but the deeper joy accompanying the realization that God's power of love has overcome the unspeakable evil that Jesus had faced on what Christians call Good Friday.

But the joyous spirit of the service was suddenly broken. Just as Betty Dunlop completed the reading of the New Testament lesson for the day, a loud, angry voice came down from the balcony. Looking up from my seat behind the pulpit, I saw a figure running down one of the aisles of the crowded balcony at the rear of the church. I cannot today remember exactly what the young man was shouting. It was obviously directed at President Clinton, who was seated in his usual pew, three rows back from the pulpit. The angry voice said something like, "Save your prayers for Bill Clinton who . . . ," and there followed a bitter denunciation of what the shouter regarded as inadequacies in the president's policies to combat AIDS (policies that actually had been more far-reaching than anything before his administration). The upbeat mood of the congregation changed to real fear. Who could tell what might come next as the young man came to the edge of the balcony?

I don't know how one can plan to react to such happenings. My instincts sent me into the pulpit where I might be able to engage this person in conversation. I waited there for a few moments to see whether he would subside. His tirade lasted, I suppose, for only half a minute, before a couple of sturdy-looking men took him in tow, escorting him back up the balcony aisle and out of sight. I took these "escorts" to be Secret Service agents; only later did I learn that they were men of our own congregation. From my vantage point in the pulpit I looked out on the shocked congregation. Two Secret Service agents had stood up behind the president and first lady, shielding them with their own bodies. The president and first lady themselves took it all in stride. Others in the congregation may have expected violence to erupt. The Easter spirit had been broken.

I spoke quietly to the congregation about the young man who had disrupted our service. He needed our prayers, I said. Don't leave the sanctuary today without offering a prayer for him. I should have voiced a prayer myself, but lacking the presence of mind to offer that spiritual leadership, I retreated to my seat. Fighting back real tears of sadness over the violence of the world that had broken into this service of joy, I frantically thought about how I could recast the introduction to my sermon on "Profound Joy." The choir began singing its gradual, an anthem that precedes the sermon. As the gradual came to an end, I was still wrapped in thought. One of the choir members, Claudia Finney, turned around to face me and said quietly, "Phil, you're on!" So I went back into the pulpit and began my sermon, speaking to a still fearful congregation. That first Easter did not begin on a joyous note, I said. All of the fear, all of the tragedy of the world had broken the lives of those early followers of Jesus. Their Lord had been crucified, dead, and buried. It was all over. There was no joy there, only despair. It was into exactly that mood of despair that the realization of the resurrection brought something totally unexpected. Today, I said, we have experienced something of the world's despair in our midst. The resurrection is most real to us when we see it in relation to this brokenness.

People still talk about that service, the one time when real disruption occurred in the eight years of presidential attendance at Foundry. It was a kind of wake-up call for the Secret Service itself, for they had in fact only had a single agent covering a balcony full of two hundred people. For the rest of us, it was a deeper lesson about the anger and brokenness in the world that tests the reality and power of the love we proclaim.

Faced on rare occasions with demonstrations or picketing outside the church—usually by groups seeking exposure before the ubiquitous television cameras, we had reason to fear further disruptions of our services. What would we do if several dozen demonstrators decided to bring their protests inside? The Secret Service people made clear that they would respond, physically if necessary, to any threat to the president himself, but legally they were not authorized to intervene simply to preserve order. The District of Columbia police had the authority to help us preserve order, but only at our request. On at least one occasion, the D.C. police urged us to give them permission to handle disruptions by arresting those who were disorderly. We hadn't yet experienced that (except for that one Easter), but it was always a possibility. Still, the last thing we wanted was an image of people being dragged bodily out of our services. What would that say about the integrity of our faith and the power of our love? So we did not give the police permission to arrest anybody in our church, nor did we respond to any suggestion that some questionable people should be kept from coming in. Our view was that this is a church in which all are welcome, and we intended to stick with that principle as long as humanly possible. I suppose we might have drawn the line if disruptions had occurred week after week. In that event, our own religious liberty as a congregation would have been on the line, and we might legitimately have asked the state (meaning the D.C. police department) to protect us in the exercise of our right. But it never came to that.

Eileen and I actually did have a game plan to deal with loud and uncontrollable disruption: I would remind the congregation that we are singing Methodists. Nobody has the ability to outshout a great singing congregation, backed up by the power of our great Casavant pipe organ! In the back of my pulpit hymnal I had several hymn numbers written out for easy reference, and we were always prepared to transform the planned service into a hymn sing—to the glory of God, of course. But thanks be to God, Eileen and I never had to utilize our contingency plan. I say "thanks be to God" with some precision, because I really think there were occasions when God's spirit, alive in this congregation, may well have prevented things from happening. On one occasion, I saw a group of our people embracing some angry visitors in an obvious display of love. Only years later, I learned that the leader of a well-known extremist (my designation) group had come into the service and had been surprised by the beautiful spirit he found there.

Looking back across the years, I want to give high marks to the Foundry congregation for its resiliency in facing the inconveniences and not allowing anxieties about possible incidents to diminish the normal flow of our services. Occasionally I tried to voice my appreciation to the congregation, sometimes kidding them along. Every six or eight weeks, on a Sunday when the Clintons were not present, I would thank the congregation for its patience. I would observe that we sometimes have to do extraordinary things in order to preserve the ordinary. Once in a while a particular incident would cause some members of the church to feel that they had been inconvenienced too much or treated disrespectfully. But those incidents were rare and, as I have said, the Secret Service was very responsive to our suggestions.

On the whole, we were able to preserve the ordinary. The Clintons didn't wish to be made over. This was one time, in the midst of a busy week, when they could sing the hymns, say the prayers, and be ordinary people in the presence of other ordinary people and the God whom we had all gathered to worship. Only very rarely was their presence even mentioned. Not that it had to be, of course! But if special note of their presence had been voiced regularly, that would have transformed a service of worship into something else. There were a few occasions when it seemed relevant to our worship to acknowledge their presence more directly. One of these was on the day after Yitzhak Rabin's assassination, when President Clinton was to fly to Israel right after the service to attend the Israeli prime minister's funeral. I voiced our shared feeling that he was going as representative of all of us and as an emissary of peace. On another occasion, just before his inauguration to a second term, I spoke of the challenges he faced in providing leadership to the nation and world and prayed God's blessing upon him and his family. On these and a handful of other occasions, it seemed appropriate to remind us all of his special vocation and our own participation in it with him. But most of the time, the Clintons were among us like any other worshipers.

Dilemmas in Preaching to the Powerful

That is not to say, however, that a preacher can be unaware of the presence of possibly the most powerful leader on earth, sitting three rows in front of the pulpit. Sometimes I have been asked whether I tailored my sermons to the president. The correct answer is that I preached exactly the same regardless of whether he was there or not. In a sense that is true, for only rarely did I know in advance that he would be in the congregation. A more candid answer is more complex. What kind of a preacher is it who doesn't speak to the uniqueness of the actual congregation that he or she faces? Could you preach to a congregation made up of farmers and totally ignore the problems of a farm population? On the other hand, if you were a preacher in the South Bronx, would you draw your illustrations and applications from Iowa farmland? Or if your congregation was made up of Eastern Shore Maryland watermen, would you ignore the peculiar situation of fisherfolk? One need only consult the parables of Jesus to find a model of how to address people in their own cultural situation in a relevant way! The fishermen. The shepherds. The farmers. The widows. The sojourners and travelers.

So if you have the president or other politically powerful people on hand, do you disregard their life situation altogether? I believe that would be to turn the gospel message into a kind of spiritual abstraction, remote from life as it is actually lived.

Moreover, the issues and problems facing the politically powerful are not just their business; they are *everybody's* business! A large majority of those present in a typical congregation are also citizens. As such, they need to be challenged to think more deeply and more clearly about citizenship as a vocation, common to all. Thus, whenever I addressed public issues from the pulpit my message was not much influenced by whether or not the president was in the congregation.

I must confess that there were occasions when I *hoped* he would be there, given the issues I intended to include in the sermon. If he was not, there was no reason to change the content of the message, since it could be and was addressed to everybody in their role as citizens. During the summer of 1993, for example, after President Clinton had been in church four or five times, it was widely reported that he was preparing an executive order to modify the exclusion of gays in the armed forces. I had not dealt much with gay rights before that time, but I felt it important to speak to this issue. I wanted to reinforce the president's intention in the face of the considerable opposition that was developing. In fact, he was not present the particular Sunday I included the issue in my sermon. While I was mildly disappointed that he wasn't there, his absence did not affect the content of the sermon at all.

A preacher who often speaks to the powerful needs to reflect on what it means to "speak truth to power." That expression, commonly voiced by Christians who are deeply concerned about issues of peace and justice, has an adversarial tone. It is as though the preacher, who is a custodian of truth, is charged with responsibility to force the powerful to confront the truths they would prefer to avoid. Sometimes that is indeed the situation. There is a grand tradition of preachers and spiritual confessors pushing the mighty to face up to their moral obligations. Think of Nathan confronting David with his "You are the man!" Or the prophet Elijah speaking truth to King Ahab and Queen Jezebel.

Although later in my pastoral journey I would have a role, as preacher and spiritual counselor, in a presidential crisis, in the earlier years, frankly, my "speaking truth to power" was usually a matter of reinforcing the president's own higher values and convictions. I didn't disagree with him at all, for instance, on the need to establish some form of universal health care. I quite concurred on the need for the United States, as the world's remaining superpower, to play a leading international role and not retreat (as some were tempted to do) into isolationism. I believed in his efforts to increase the minimum wage. I agreed that the United States should take a leadership role in increasing world trade. All of these points were, in my opinion, factually relevant expressions of the faith we shared in common. In other words, these were not simply secular matters, having no place in the context of faith and worship. I will say more in a subsequent chapter about the problems of addressing real issues. But in relation to President Clinton, I simply did not often disagree with the main directions of his thinking.

I was troubled, however, by his policy on welfare reform. He had come into office with an announced intention of changing welfare as we know it. What could that mean? I had been a student of welfare policies dating back into the 1960s, when one of my earliest books on economic ethics was on the then hotly debated idea of a "guaranteed annual income."[1] As the president's thinking emerged more clearly in early 1996, it became evident that he thought welfare reform meant getting as many people off the welfare roles as possible and into gainful employment. I agreed that large numbers of welfare recipients had become too dependent upon welfare grants and that this was diminishing them as persons, but at the same time it seemed that many of the proponents of welfare reform were primarily interested in cutting public expenses and that abandoning the community's responsibility to care for its neediest members would achieve that shortsighted goal. I worried that a highly individualistic, moralistic, and competitive ethic—utterly remote from the gospel as I understood it—was behind the thinking of many advocates of welfare reform. And the argument that private charitable giving is the morally fitting response to poverty—rather than public expenditures and programs struck me simply as a way for prosperous and self-centered people to avoid what should be a shared responsibility of the whole society.

Still, the existing welfare system was clearly chaotic. Support levels varied greatly among the states. It was usually difficult for persons to move toward economic independence without risking an abrupt loss of the income on which they were dependent. In most states, the support levels themselves were so low that welfare recipients were trapped in poverty. I concluded that work incentives were more important than I had earlier thought in my enthusiasm for the guaranteed annual income.

When the issue was before Congress in the summer of 1996, I privately applauded (but not from the pulpit) the president's vetoing more draconian forms of welfare reform, and I did not feel clear enough in my own thinking to oppose outright the bill that he eventually signed. I did address the issue from the pulpit, and in his hearing, that if people are to be required to work then there simply must be available jobs. It is not enough to assume that the jobs will be there if people are forced off the welfare rolls, and I was pleased when President Clinton made a similar point in his acceptance speech at the 1996 Democratic National Convention. Of course, it also follows that available jobs need to be at wage levels commensurate with a decent standard of living.

My convictions and the president's seemed most directly in conflict on capital punishment. In common with my United Methodist denomina-

1. J. Philip Wogaman, *Guaranteed Annual Income: The Moral Issues* (Nashville: Abingdon Press, 1968).

tion, I oppose the death penalty. Throughout his public career, President Clinton (in common with most high officials) has supported it. On a couple of occasions he was present when I spoke directly or indirectly on that subject—once to tell the poignant story of the brother of a murder victim who appealed to the governor of Virginia to spare the life of the murderer. As reported in the press, this brother's statement was simple and beautiful in its affirmation of deeper human values and in his compassion even for the one who had deprived him of his sister. In concluding that story, I acknowledged that I didn't know whether I would have had that much grace if the victim had been one of my own loved ones. But, I said, "I do not doubt that his appeal was straight from the heart of God."

I do not think my preaching voiced any "party line," nor was it designed to please politically powerful people, like the president, who were there. Sometimes I pushed the envelope, as the saying goes, in directions with which the president and others might have been in disagreement. I can record, however, that at no time in those eight years did either the president or first lady ever seek to influence what was said or not said in the pulpit. Given the pressures they were under from religious conservatives on such issues as gay rights, I found that noteworthy and commendable.

I don't want to make all this sound too easy. Knowing that the president might be present certainly helped keep me on my toes. I felt considerable self-imposed pressure to say the right thing at the right time. That should be the objective of every preacher in mounting any pulpit. But the prospect of preaching to the president and others in the diverse Foundry congregation in those years certainly raised the pressure a notch or two. A certain amount of nervousness can be the preacher's friend rather than his or her adversary. It can help focus the mind and generate energy. It can also help us avoid complacency in preparation for preaching. I never waited until Saturday to prepare a sermon; a sermon has to have more time to develop. But there were times when the thing just wouldn't seem to jell. I don't even want to remember how many Saturday nights there were when I still didn't feel I had it quite right—and how many Sunday afternoons when the right way to say something suddenly dawned on me, an hour or so too late.

The presence of a president probably moves the alertness of a whole congregation up a few degrees. This greatly facilitates communication, of course. It isn't necessary then (if it ever is) to use rhetorical tricks and corny jokes to get people's attention. But it also means that one must be as accurate as possible with facts and, insofar as this is possible, be humble about alternative viewpoints. I say more about this in chapter 6.

One of the little prayers I often used privately before entering the service is from the Episcopal *Book of Common Prayer*. It includes these words: "Bless and direct, we beseech thee Lord, those who in this our generation speak where many listen and write what many read; that they may do their part in making the heart of this people wise, its mind sound, and its will righteous; to the honor of Jesus Christ our Lord." At first blush, that prayer seems an invitation to take oneself a bit too seriously. Basking in one's own importance as one who speaks "where many listen," one forgets how quickly our words can be forgotten. (At least, sometimes I hope my words will be quickly forgotten!) The deeper point is that our words *deserve* to be forgotten if they do not nourish the spirit and will of those who listen. I must add that some of the most exciting times for me as preacher occurred when facing a very small congregation—for example, at the Wednesday evening Communion and healing services where I occasionally preached and where fewer than thirty people were generally present. It can be exciting to preach before a great congregation including prominent and powerful people. But I have learned that the same excitement can grip us when it is given to us to preach a helpful word to a very small congregation of people who are not prominent or powerful. Clearly that means that authentic communication of the gospel and its application to life transcends more superficial distinctions. I am reminded that Jesus himself did not speak in a "megachurch," and that he did not have a television or radio ministry—and that he did not preach to Caesar!

I was intrigued, as a pastor, to observe the effect this famous family had upon other people in the church. I can recall occasions when the president or first lady responded with great human warmth and sensitivity to individuals who were obviously emotionally needy in some way or another—and when there could have been no conceivable political advantage. That helped me to provide my own support for such people. I recall the joy of one elderly person, confined with severe arthritis to a room in a modest nursing home, when she received a Christmas card personally signed by the Clintons, who had taken part in a card-signing event we had organized for members of the congregation. She kept that card pinned to her bulletin board for years. And there was the terminally ill woman with a speech handicap in whom the Clintons took special interest. These were people who had no political influence whatsoever.

Occasionally the youth directors scheduled informal conversation sessions that were designed to facilitate communication between the youth and their parents, partly on the theory that young people could hear things better from parents other than their own and, more importantly, that parents could get the message more clearly from other parents' children. These were always interesting and productive meetings. Since Chelsea Clinton was an active member of the youth groups, junior high and senior high, her parents participated right alongside the other parents and their children. The youth and their parents were generally invited to one of the White House Christmas parties, often emerging with colorful stories.

The presence of the first family affected greatly the life of the church and my own ministry during those years. How different would the church and that ministry have been had they not come that snow-covered Sunday in 1993 and then become regulars? I frankly do not know. There was so much more to the church in those years and so many more aspects to my pastoral journey there. I imagine our experience would not have been drastically different. Still, their presence broadened the church's opportunities for service and deepened our sense of the humanity of people at all levels of society. That affected us all.

Chapter Four

Learning to Be a Pastor

In which I learn afresh what it means to be a real pastor—overcome absurd fears of hospital visitation—discover that being a pastor to people is not primarily in the office setting—experience the gift and burden of trust—try to be a pastor to youth—become inspired by how God works in the lives of people, sometimes quite unexpectedly—learn how pastoral care is less a one-on-one interaction between a pastor and an individual parishioner and more an expression of mutual caring in a community of faith

For sheer enjoyment, I suppose I found the disciplines and excitements of preaching more satisfying than anything else about ministry. I freely confess the element of vanity lurking in that, although preaching is also where I felt most challenged to use whatever God-given gifts I possess. I didn't aspire to be a pulpit prima donna and probably had no aptitude for that anyway. But, whether or not a preacher is so gifted, even the best pulpit oratory rings hollow if it is not backed up by a caring pastoral ministry. How else is one to know the people to whom one is speaking? So, as I entered into my new life at Foundry, I knew that I could not just be a preacher; I had also to be a pastor.

Hospital Visitation

I soon discovered that some of my initial apprehensions about hospital visitation were utterly unfounded. I confess I had dreaded hospital visits more than anything. It wasn't that I didn't want to go; it was more that I feared that my visits would not be welcomed, that they would be an intrusion upon people who were suffering enough already. I'm sure that most pastors who are more experienced than I was would find that humorous, but my apprehensions were real enough to me. Of course, what I discovered was exactly the reverse. Looking back across my ten years at Foundry, I am hard-pressed to think of even one time when I was not welcomed warmly and appreciatively.

Why was that so? I would like to think it is because of my scintillating personality. But in truth, that isn't it at all! When in hospital, people are generally confronting a fairly serious illness or injury, accompanied often by sheer physical pain, sometimes by emotional pains and anxieties. The presence of a pastor—really, any pastor—symbolizes the gift of God's grace. That means that prayer is especially welcomed. That can mean prayers or prayerlike poetry (such as some of the Psalms) that have been written by others and are timeless in their appeal, or it can mean prayers spontaneously spoken by the pastor at the bedside (which was usually my practice).

Something else is often at work when people receive a hospital visit from their pastor: He or she, like it or not, symbolizes the whole church community of which pastor and parishioner are a part. There is a sense in which the pastor's presence embodies the whole church. That may sound pretentious, but again and again I have sensed such a feeling on the part of a parishioner in a hospital setting. I sometimes invited that perception with words like these: "Our whole congregation would like to be here, to offer words of support and encouragement. But since there isn't enough space in this room for more than a thousand people, they sent me as their representative." We laughed about that together, because of course a large majority of the congregation wouldn't even know this patient, much less that she or he was in the hospital. But in a larger sense, we could still feel that the congregation had indeed commissioned me to be present in such a setting and that they were all implicitly present in spirit.

Because Foundry people live in all parts of this large metropolitan area, the pastoral staff visited parishioners in more than two dozen different hospitals—ranging from the Inova Fairfax and Springfield hospitals in Virginia, to the Prince George's or Annapolis hospitals in Maryland, to the great military hospitals, Walter Reed and Bethesda Naval, to nearby university hospitals such as George Washington, Georgetown, and Howard. This may seem like a daunting array of hospital visitations, but we rarely had more than two or three people in hospital during any one week (and sometimes we didn't know a parishioner was in hospital until later). I tried personally to visit every parishioner known to be in a hospital, and over the years I'm sure I did in a majority of cases.

I had also wondered whether I might encounter bureaucratic difficulties in getting in to see hospitalized parishioners. Again, the fears were unfounded. In almost every case I was able to go straight in to have a word of prayer with a parishioner even in an intensive care unit. In fact, I discovered that a pastor can often visit an intensive care patient even when the family is not yet allowed in, and that a pastor is not generally limited to the published visiting hours. Hospital staffs seem to understand that spiritual undergirding genuinely helps in the healing process. The church-related hospitals, such as the United Methodist-related Sibley Hospital or the Roman Catholics' Holy Cross, Providence, or Georgetown University hospitals, were predictably receptive and accommodating. But the same was true of secular hospitals such as the Washington Hospital Center or Suburban Hospital in Montgomery County, Maryland.

There were also times when I made a hospital visit more out of a sense of obligation than desire. I just wasn't in the mood. But invariably, something about the setting changed everything. It was as if I was the one being energized more than the patient in the room.

That happened one night when I least expected it. A patient had died at George Washington University Hospital. I did not know this elderly Chinese woman or any of the members of the extended family of which she had been the matriarch. I was awakened from a sound sleep at about 2:00 A.M. on a Saturday night by a call from the hospital's emergency ward. Could I come be with the family? I was not their pastor, but they had been unable to reach that minister or any other United Methodist minister. But I was listed in the D.C. phone directory, so they had called me. At 2:00 A.M., and on a night before I was supposed to preach! I was, I confess, really quite angry. Nevertheless, out of a sense of sheer obligation or something like that, I mumbled my assent, quickly dressed, and headed out to the car. I do not want to describe any further the mood I was in, other than to say that only by the grace of God did I manage to avoid an accident as I sped down Massachusetts Avenue toward the hospital. Upon arrival, I was quickly introduced to the large grieving family. Their obvious sorrow, the obvious spiritual need, the expectancy with which they turned to me, all dissipated my anger like the mists of dawn before the rising sun. I talked with them for a while, learning more about their family and about this loved one who was now gone. We spoke of our shared faith. I prayed with them, trusting that God would forgive me my anger enough to inspire a prayer that might help. Perhaps these moments did help; I'll never know. I do know that it helped my own spiritual centering. And as for my sermon the next morning, whatever effect the loss of sleep had caused seemed more than offset by the deeper levels of spiritual energy released.

Trying to be a pastor to people in the midst of their need has that effect. It is also inspiring to see people respond to truly awful physical conditions with extraordinary courage and resiliency. Here was Richard Lord, not quite fifty, suffering from a rare disorder that affects internal organs. For reasons too complex for me to relate—or fully understand—he was required to lie flat on his back in a suburban hospital for weeks, with little to do but stare at the ceiling. He was, throughout this time, wonderfully supported by his wife, Nina, and their family. I found his spirit to be remarkably resilient. His life could not, in the end, be saved. But what a legacy he left to his loved ones and to those of us privileged to serve him in small ways.

Spending so much time in hospitals taught me to always try to be responsive in totally unanticipated situations. Late one night, after having prayer with a parishioner at Sibley Hospital in northwest Washington, I was on my way through the darkened lobby area downstairs when I was approached by a couple of men. Did I know where the hospital chaplain could be found? I pointed toward his office, by the chapel off the lobby, but thought he would be gone by that hour. We approached the office together and, as I had expected, it was locked up for the night. I am also a Christian minister, I told them; can I help you in some way? One of the men said his wife was terminally ill. She was in a coma and was not expected to live through the night. Could I go up to her room with him and say a prayer for her? Of course I could. As we waited for the elevator, something in the appearance of the two men led me to ask whether they were Muslims. Yes, they acknowledged. I said that would not matter. We got to the room. Numbers of people, whom I took to be relatives, were in the hallway and in the woman's room. Everybody crowded in, surrounding her bed. I am no judge of such things, but from the woman's appearance and labored breathing I suspected that she indeed might not live through the night. I asked those present what was the direction of Mecca. Like a compass needle pointing north, hands indicated what they must have thought was the exact direction of the Muslim holy city. I said I thought I understood the importance of that to them. At the same time, I added, Allah, or God, is all-powerful and all-merciful, so we could think of God's presence in the room beside us, looking upon their loved one with greatest compassion. I offered prayer, then, invoking God's blessing upon this dying woman and God's kindness and consolation to her loved ones. I do not remember my exact words, but when I had finished I held their attention for a few more moments. I identified myself as a Christian minister and said this was the first time I had ever had prayer with Muslims in this way. But I had felt the compassionate presence of the God who is greater than all of us there in that room.

I have no way to know when the woman actually died, nor what happened to her husband and the rest of her family. I did feel a kinship with all of them, even in that brief time, and a deeper sense of a presence that transcends the lines of religious narrowness that so often divide us.

Sometimes hospital visitation can drain a pastor's own spiritual energy. That can be especially true when spending time with deeply depressed people. On several occasions, I needed to visit young people in hospital treatment wards for the emotionally depressed. It was usually hard for them to respond much. I learned that it was enough just to be there for them and to offer some reassuring words and prayer. Only later, if ever, would I learn whether this had been helpful.

Perhaps not surprisingly, the longer I was at Foundry, the more people came to me with emotional, spiritual, or relational problems. Did I feel prepared to help them? Not really. Some of what I had learned in seminary long ago about pastoral counseling was moderately helpful. In all honesty, I'd have to say that most was not. The basic model was therapeutic, as though a pastor was some kind of psychological therapist—without the intensive training of most therapists but with a built-in constituency of psychologically needy people. In my course work and clinical pastoral training, the operative theories were patterned, more or less, on the late Carl Rogers's "client centered therapy." This was supposed to be nondirective, keyed almost entirely to the "client's" own expressions. The lingering value in this was, I found, to try to be a good listener, helping the person express feelings and describe the difficulties as he or she was encountering them. The shortcoming lay, it seemed to me, in inhibiting me from offering positive words of encouragement and support.

Also, I do not remember anything in those long-ago classes and clinical training experiences about how a pastor can help people by praying with them. Most pastors have learned that prayer can be a resource of great significance. Through prayer we can pour out together our pain and anxieties, and through prayer we can discover afresh the tender grace of God. A prayer hymn by Amy W. Carmichael, which I have sometimes voiced with people suffering in terminal illness, expresses the hope that even when there is no prospect for relief of pain, the Lord will "come near" to grant peace at a deeper level. I have made it a practice also to offer a prayer of thanks for the care and skill of health care providers. There are, of course, biblical resources such as the Psalms that are especially helpful.

Still, I know my limitations in the counseling department well enough to avoid pretense. I am not equipped, either by training or practical experience, to be a therapist! When confronting a serious emotional or relational problem, I felt my best contribution was to help people connect with better-trained professionals. In any event, a busy pastor simply does not have time to have extended regular counseling sessions with the same person. If it seemed evident that a person needed to be helped by a series of pastoral conferences extending over a period of weeks or months, I generally found a way to pass this responsibility on to others. There may be valid exceptions to this rule, but in my ministry at least they were real exceptions.

Bringing the Best Out of People

These stories, and dozens more, are mostly about helping people in their need—sometimes about helping people in pain find new wholeness. Perhaps there is a sense in which this is typical of pastoral care.

Yet to be a pastor means much more than helping physically or emotionally sick people. It can be about relating to people on the basis of their strengths, helping them think through major decisions, encouraging them to find new possibilities. Sometimes it is simply to be a trusted friend, with whom one can interact about the things that matter most in life.

Occasionally such pastoral interactions occur in the pastor's office. But I was amazed to discover how much of this happened, so to speak, "on the run." There might be a conversation before or after a church meeting. Sometimes a few moments shared immediately after a Sunday morning worship service could be highly significant. Occasionally it would be a phone call, ostensibly about something else but actually loaded with deeper contents.

As a pastor, I tried to be alert to events of major importance in the lives of people—a personal success, a new job, the loss of a job, things happening to the children of parishioners, the social concerns and causes in which a parishioner might be deeply engaged. While Foundry is not a megachurch, it is large enough to make it impossible for anyone to keep up with everything happening to everybody. As one of my own seminary professors used to say, it's the batting average that counts. It is not everything versus nothing; it is more is better than less.

The pastoral interactions with young people were among the most satisfying during my Foundry years. They weren't easy, however. As a downtown church, drawing people from all parts of a very wide metropolitan area, it was virtually impossible to schedule youth fellowship meetings at times other than Sunday mornings. That meant that I was generally tied up at what would have been the prime times for the youth. There were occasional youth retreats or "lock-ins" (times when the youth would bring their sleeping bags and spend a night and a day in the church building). My involvements with these were, at best, marginal. There were the confirmation classes, a part of which Carolyn and I participated in but which were mostly the responsibility of our minister of Christian education.

Then there was the annual youth participation in the Appalachian Service Project (ASP). The church invested a good deal of energy and no small amount of money in ASP. This program resembles Habitat for Humanity. Every year, teams of youth from Foundry, accompanied by adult sponsors, spend a week repairing and renovating the modest homes of poor families in the Appalachian Mountain region. It is a two-way street: The Appalachian families get some badly needed help, while the youth discover human values in a very different setting and incidentally acquire some practical skills in a variety of maintenance tasks. Both the youth and their sponsors find this a wonderfully bonding experience. During three summers (1993, 1994, and 1996) Carolyn and I were privileged to accompany the youth and to develop, even in the course of a few days, some very meaningful relationships, which had positive spillover effects in subsequent years, even affecting our relationships with youth who didn't go on the trips. Perhaps it helped for the youth to see the one whom they had only viewed in the pulpit now helping dig holes for new footings, fitting and nailing siding in place, spreading tar for a new roof, or yelling when a hammer hit his thumb instead of a nail. I learned that participating in a common activity enormously facilitates communication on other things.

The experience also helped the youth grow in their appreciation of people different from themselves. Our young people, who had grown up in a major metropolitan area, came to see life through the eyes of rural people in a mountainous region. While we were there to help, this was not simply a one-way street. The youth (and the adult sponsors) picked up a whole lot about life from the mountain people, including their love of the land, their relationships with their children, their quiet dignity, even some practical skills—such as those of a disabled man who could still coach our youth in basic carpentry, and those of another man who, having captured a poisonous copperhead snake, taught us about that aspect of life in the mountains.

There was some unusual drama the year Chelsea Clinton was in the program. Her participation meant, of course, that the Secret Service was involved. We must have presented quite a scene as our caravan of three vans, loaded with youth and counselors, proceeded down the highway followed by a couple of SUVs with Secret Service aboard. The home Chelsea's group was to work on was chosen for the usual reasons of need, but also with an eye toward security considerations. The family was not informed at first about who they had digging away under their house and playing with their children, but the SUV parked down the dirt road created anxieties, and so we had to tell them the president's daughter was working on their house. Imagine their reaction! It was all taken in stride, however, but this young woman worked her heart out as we dug away to make space for a new foundation under this simple mountain home. Carolyn and I were also fascinated to observe how the other youth, from Foundry and two other churches, protected Chelsea from intrusions on her privacy.[1]

Being Pastor to a Whole Community

One of the main problems with conventional conceptions of the pastoral role is that the role is so often framed individualistically—a pastor's relationship with specific persons. At worst, this is a vision limited to conferences scheduled during office hours in the pastor's study—valuable though such conferences can sometimes be. Even at its best, an individualistic conception misses the broadly communal character of a church. The larger pastoral vision is of a community of mutually caring people, vastly magnifying what any one person could possibly do. Thus, it may be that the pastor's single most important task is to cultivate a spiritual climate in which people are deeply involved in caring about and for one another.

From my first Sunday in 1992 until the end of my Foundry years in 2002, I borrowed an idea from my crosstown colleague Bill Holmes to help cultivate an attitude of community in the congregation. During the announcements section of the worship service, I noted those from the church who were known to be in hospitals, or facing the loss of loved ones, or recently married—events on such a level of importance. Then I asked

1. I want to add that, while this was a presidential election year, her parents did nothing to exploit their daughter's presence in this undertaking. Quite the contrary, they did everything they could to ensure that no notice would be taken. Despite this, it leaked out through the local police of the mountain community and became a news item in Kentucky newspapers.

for somebody to volunteer to communicate with each person. And then I waited until a volunteer's hand went up. On the rare occasions when no one quickly volunteered, I reminded people that the service simply could not go on until somebody accepted that responsibility. Their involvement was not usually a substitute for my own or that of another staff person but an indication of the caring of the whole congregation. In fact, it could sometimes be especially meaningful to a person in hospital or otherwise in need if the person who volunteered to get in touch was a total stranger. That *really* made the point that this was the congregation, as community, lending its friendly support.

It is amazing to me that a large, diverse congregation, gathered from different parts of a great metropolitan area—a congregation that seemingly would be quite impersonal—could accept the invitation to respond in such a personal way. From day one there was almost no criticism of this practice. Indeed, over and over I heard appreciative comments from people, including visitors to the church. People began reporting situations to us, expecting the announcement and recruitment of volunteers to follow. Occasionally, once in a long while, someone having surgery or some such thing would specifically request that this not be announced, and we scrupulously followed that direction. (I will confess that I came to understand that not everybody filing that kind of request really meant it, and so I might pursue that person's real intentions further.)

If this kind of program can be pulled off successfully in a large downtown church in a great city, where could it not be done? I suppose a megachurch with thousands of people in the sanctuary might have to find a different method. But we could do it with six or seven hundred people present at a time. Certainly this would be workable in a smaller church in a more homogeneous cultural setting.

The climate of mutual sharing in pastoral ministry evolved in other ways as well. The minister of the parish, Walter Shropshire, developed a form of the Stephen Ministry at Foundry, recruiting and training numbers of laypersons for specialized assigned pastoral relationships with persons in various kinds of need. Carolyn participated actively in this and, because she was also my spouse, I found her pastoral involvements very helpful personally. We were very careful to preserve pastoral confidences, but we discovered in time that people would share things with her, expecting her to pass them on to me—and sometimes vice versa. Married pastors and spouses have a wide variety of relationships with parishes, and for many this kind of pastoral relationship would be neither feasible nor desired. But it was helpful in our case.

There are, of course, other kinds of approaches to a communal sharing of the pastoral responsibility. One that is typical of successful large churches is the development of small groups, designed for mutual spiritual sharing and study and for common action. Methodists will recognize the Wesleyan roots of the "class meetings," cell groups developed by the early Methodists for such purposes. In contemporary United Methodist circles, the development of Covenant Discipleship groups and the Disciple program greatly facilitate an atmosphere of shared spiritual life and mutual caring. Foundry has a number of such groups and a variety of mission groups charged with helping the homeless, the hungry, victims of AIDS, and other persons in need, as well as expressing the church's concerns for peace and human rights. No one person could participate in all of these, of course. But we have encouraged everybody to be involved in some small-group activity and not limit church participation to attendance in the large services. Each of the church's equipping ministers has responsibility for a variety of groups. While the groups have measurable objectives, the more intangible aspects of mutual caring are very often a central part of the picture.

It would, I suppose, be easy to dismiss much of this as merely sociological—as representing the kind of social values that could be expected in any social group or institution that people find meaningful. What does it have to do with the church's raison d'être?

Certainly the kinds of pastoral encounters I mentioned earlier in this chapter have obvious spiritual dimensions. Is that also true of getting people to look after one another in groups, or even in the recruitment of volunteers in the great congregation? Maybe not. Now and again one encounters people in the church whose participation and even motivations seem unaffected by theological conviction. A mission group devoted to hands-on ministry to people in need can be conducted without reference to a specific faith commitment. Indeed, it would distort the integrity of some kinds of good works to attach them too rigidly to such commitments. Homeless people who come to the church's Friday morning "walk in" time—when specific needs of the people are addressed—should not have to profess (or feign) the faith of the church as a condition of receiving the church's help.

Yet it seems clear to me that theological context is crucial. My pastoral journey at Foundry deepened my conviction that pastoral ministry, both in its individual and its communal forms, is above all an expression of God's grace. It is because of what we have been given that we, in turn, can give. Without that sense of God's love, it is easy for burnout to sap one's drive after initial enthusiasm has run its course. Some readers will recall a campaign that was promoted some years ago called "Hands across America," with a human chain of people holding hands at a particular time all across the land. It didn't exactly cover the whole country as intended, but the concomitant effort to raise funds for people in need had some measurable effect. A year or so later, the leader of this effort was asked about follow-up. His response was that, for the time being, at least, people were suffering from what he called "compassion fatigue" and were no longer involved. That is a nice term for what I am speaking about. Without a deeper spiritual undergirding, grounded in real love, it is easy for compassion fatigue to set in.

A deeper sense of God's grace helps also to undergird the commitment by a congregation to be inclusive, without the usual cultural distinctions that lead to the exclusion of unwanted people. In our church we had a rare opportunity to express more clearly what that means, for we had, at once, some of the most prominent people in the nation and some of its most deprived. By emphasizing our common gift of God's grace, we could make clear that all belong together in a community of mutual care.

Confronted by the actual, not only the theoretical, demands of pastoral ministry, I became increasingly impatient with the judgmental attitudes of some fellow Christians (if that is not itself too judgmental a thing to say!). We have to make moral distinctions, of course, but it is all too easy to slip into condemning those of whose behavior we disapprove. I became all the more appreciative of Paul's distinction between trust in God's grace and self-righteousness based upon external performance. It is not that performance doesn't matter; it is that love is the ground of motivation and the criterion by which we assess performance. It became increasingly clear to me that you cannot be a pastor to people if you don't love them. But a pastor can grow in that love, just as a congregation can grow in the mutual love that enables the whole body to be pastoral.

Chapter Five

Coping with Death

In which I confront the grim reality that all of us must die—see how different people respond to this in different ways—learn some of the special problems this poses for pastoral ministry and how death is somehow different in the church setting—help survivors find healing

A pastor has the burden and privilege of being present to people at the times when their faith and even their humanity are most seriously tested. Many, even of those who appear most self-sufficient, are brought face-to-face with their limitations when confronted by life-threatening illness or the loss of loved ones in death. A pastor is also tested by those moments, for many people turn to a pastor in search of the encouragements and consolations of deeper faith. As a pastor, I never looked forward to such times. I didn't want people to die; I didn't want relationships and families to be broken by the loss of beloved friends, spouses, and family members. I didn't want to be pushed to my own limits when called upon to minister to people who were facing theirs. But I quickly discovered that there are resources in our faith that undergird pastors, and I always took those times seriously.

Of course, my first personal encounters with death came long before I began ministry at Foundry at age sixty. I lost my mother to a brain tumor, following an extended period of suffering, when I was only sixteen. My father died suddenly from a heart attack when I was twenty-seven. I already knew something about the deep pain of losing people who are as close to you as life itself. Even professionally, I had had more than passing encounters with death. There had been a handful of deaths and funerals in the small Massachusetts church I served for a couple of years as a graduate student. A promising young student developed a brain tumor (reminiscent of my mother) early in my teaching career at Wesley Theological Seminary. In fact, I probably learned more about real pastoral care in my clumsy attempts to be helpful to him and his wife during his years of illness and then after his death. Along the way, other friends and colleagues had suffered and died.

One of the things I learned in ministry to the student, Sam Willard, is not to try to be profound all the time. One incident lingers in my memory. Sam had just gone through a second episode of brain surgery. A day or so later, when he was regaining consciousness, I came to his hospital bedside. He seemed conscious, and seeing me he tried to speak. His slurred speech was difficult to make out, but there was a tone of urgency in his voice. "Yes, Sam," I sought to be helpful. "What is it you're trying to say?" There followed more garbled speech. "Yes, Sam," I repeated. "What is it?" More slurred speech, but with greater urgency. I was certain that he was trying to voice something from the spiritual depths about what he was facing. "Yes, Sam." I continued, seeking to voice his thoughts for him. I said something like, "I know how deeply this is affecting you and how God is becoming more real to you." Sam responded even more energetically as he sought to be understood. As though gripped by sudden new powers, he sat bolt upright in bed and demanded, "Where is the bedpan?"

Years later I found myself by the bedside of a recently retired friend and colleague who was dying of cancer. His cancer was not only terminal but very painful. I didn't even try to be profound this time but just to be present as a friend. "Phil," he said, "I have learned that a physical crisis is also a spiritual crisis. I look out across the void—it is like a great abyss—and I get no answer back." I didn't try to give him his answer back; I just tried to be a friend and to say how much we cared about him.

A few months later, shortly before his death, he summoned a number of his friends and colleagues to his room. We had a beautiful service of Communion together. We left the room, but one by one we were drawn back for a word of blessing from him. I don't remember what he said that day, but he didn't refer to that earlier conversation about the great abyss he was confronting in his pain. Somehow, in ways I will never understand, his answer had come back.

So I didn't have to wait until beginning my Foundry journey to confront pastoral issues related to death.

Death at Foundry

I did, however, have to face death in different ways as a pastor at Foundry. For one thing, as senior minister of a large congregation, I had a clear, unavoidable responsibility. When somebody in this community of faith died or faced terminal illness, it was now, so to speak, on my watch.

In fact, it came rather soon. During my first summer, a vital, seemingly healthy man in his fifties, well-known in the congregation, died suddenly after a massive heart attack. I helped the family plan the funeral service and did all I could to help his wife and family along. The details have faded from my memory, but I do remember feeling very close to them all.

Shortly after that, a young man called asking for an appointment. A friend of his had died, but since the friend had not had a church home, he wondered whether a memorial service could be held in our chapel. Yes, of course, I said. The young man then informed me, a bit apprehensively I thought, that his friend had died of AIDS. That, I reassured him, makes no difference. Of course you can have the service here. Then, he wondered, would I be willing to conduct the service? Yes, yes, I said. I'll do what I can. As the story developed, I learned that the deceased had been a bartender at JR's Bar, a focal point of Washington's gay community. His fellow workers, most of them also without church affiliation, would constitute most of the congregation. The rest of the congregation would be the deceased's family from Alabama. The contrast between these two constituencies was obvious, but if there was much tension I wasn't aware of it. The next Sunday, during the concerns period, I spoke of how our church had been in ministry to this young man who had died of AIDS. Some remarked later that it had been venturesome if not courageous of me to share this with the congregation. I hadn't given a second thought to any negative reactions and, in fact, I don't think there were any.

Other deaths, of course, followed. Upon arriving at Foundry, I learned that Susan Parker, one of the real saints of the church, had terminal cancer. Professionally, she was an oncological nurse, so she knew exactly what the score was and what to expect. I visited her several times that first autumn at Foundry. On one occasion, I expressed some anxiety to her about an issue I was facing in the church. Her searching comment to me was, "Remember it is God's church, Phil." I should be more trusting. I should see it in the deeper perspective. Of course, she was right about that, and I could not be offended by her giving me needed spiritual instruction. She thus became one of my earliest reminders that pastoral ministry is a two-way street. Often we get a lot more than we can give. Susan's own faith and courage were going to be tested by a lot of pain, she knew. To suppress the pain she would have to receive regular doses of morphine, which she could control. She made a conscious decision to keep that to the minimum so she could continue to be present, consciously and spiritually, to her family. When her death came, shortly after Christmas, the congregation gathered in celebration of a life well lived.

Sometimes the onset of terminal illness came very suddenly, with death following all too quickly. My first Sunday at Foundry, I was wandering around the chancel area near the pulpit prior to the early service. A vivacious woman in her fifties was there, busying herself with various altar guild type duties. Thrusting her hand out to me in greeting, she said, "I'm Carole Hilty. My job is to pamper the ministers." That sounded all right to me! She and her husband, a senior official in the Agriculture Department in the first Bush administration, were good friends to all of us. Then, within three months, an examination revealed that Carole had a cancer that had metastasized beyond control. Shortly after the next Easter, she was gone.

It is a painful thing for a pastor to come to know and love people in the congregation, and then to experience their death. Of course this happens, one way or another, to most people, as it had to me long before beginning my ministry at Foundry. But pastors experience this situation a good deal more often than most people, and are generally closer to the spiritual struggles that accompany illness and death.

Explaining Death

Confronted by the enormity of death, people grope for answers. We all do. Not infrequently one hears it said that God had a larger purpose. For example, we might hear that God wanted to take this little child (in the case of an obviously untimely death by disease or accident) to be with him in heaven, as though there is a divine plan in which the birth and death of every person is programmed by God. I don't know many pastors who challenge such views in the immediate aftermath of the loss of loved ones. Still, we are all going to die; that is certain. Unless we are prepared to be out-and-out determinists, there has to be room for sheer, unforeseeable accidents, or random vulnerabilities to disease, or the natural wearing down and wearing out of our bodies. While a given life may have great meaning, the particular way in which a person dies may not.

A pastor sometimes has to deal with a survivor's unwarranted blame or self-blame. At other times it may actually appear that somebody is dying because of what he or she has done or not done. This can sometimes be a part of the truth: You can inadvertently take the wrong medication. Because you drove through a particular intersection at a particular time instead of five minutes later, you are broadsided by a truck doing eighty miles an hour. These are ordinary risks we take just by getting out of bed and going through the day. But it is also true that we can die as a direct result of doing something wrong, something we shouldn't have done. I think of a clergy colleague a few years ago who drove into an intersection on a busy street without looking both ways. He was hit by a truck and killed instantly. Did he deserve to die? It was, to be sure, his "fault." He had a moral responsibility to himself and others to be a careful driver, and he let his attention lapse. But that is a far cry from saying that he deserved to *die* for that lapse of attention! Sometimes I found myself ministering to the dying or to their survivors in situations where it seemed evident that a pattern of behavior was largely responsible for the death. For instance, somebody who is overweight because of unhealthy eating habits or lack of exercise would bear some responsibility for related health problems, just as a habitual smoker's lung cancer, emphysema, or heart disease can be related to his or her smoking. Some (but not by any means all) deaths from AIDS can be related to risky behaviors.

Whatever tendency I might have had as an ethicist (or as a human being, for that matter) to look for patterns of responsibility, I certainly learned as a pastor I had to put that aside and avoid moralistic judgments. Here is, or was, a person whose life, taken as a whole, has much value. This person is not to be *defined* by whatever caused his or her death. I came to feel it would be a kind of blasphemy to treat such deaths as God's just punishment against sin. Who can say that pain and death are appropriate punishments for physically risky behaviors in a world where so many people do much worse things with impunity, bearing in mind as well that many of the victims of AIDS, cancer, and heart disease have done nothing that was directly responsible for their fate?

I recall one parishioner who died of emphysema. He had gotten hooked on smoking, I believe, during his military service in World War II. At that time, smoking was a common form of relaxation among the troops, and its dangers were unknown. Later, it became nearly impossible for many to shake the habit. I do not doubt that this man's suffering and death were a direct result of his smoking. But as I witnessed his struggle for breath in several hospitalizations and the wasting away of his body, I could not interpret his plight moralistically. He was a good man. He was a faithful, responsible leader in the church during earlier, healthier years. What I saw in his suffering absolutely convinced me of the dangers of tobacco, but nothing about it led me to condemn him personally.

In the earlier years of the disease and prior to the development of more effective treatments, we had to deal with the deaths of several victims of AIDS. Most received loving support from family members—sometimes to their surprise. Especially touching were a couple of instances when a gay person had to inform his parents and siblings that he was both gay and HIV positive. In the 1980s and early 1990s, such a diagnosis was virtually a death sentence. The end could be held at bay for a while, but after various hospitalizations and brief respites, death would come—often to a body that had become only a shadow of its former self. Pastoral ministry in such circumstances could be both compelling and difficult—compelling because of the obvious need for compassionate pastoral care, but difficult because of the complex blending of physical and spiritual pain and, often, a sense of sheer hopelessness. Most of the hope had to be at the ultimate level, in the shared confidence that come what may we belong to a loving God. That confidence did not always come easily to AIDS patients.

There was a young man dying of AIDS for whom I became a pastor. In and out of hospitals over a period of years, before some of the more successful recent treatments had been developed, he showed considerable spiritual strength. But that was severely tested at least twice. Once, as I visited him in a D.C. hospital, he related a dream he had had the night before. In the dream a menacing figure, whom he identified as demonic, had threatened to take hold of him. He had wrestled free. But now he worried that this might happen again. If it does, I said, you tell this devil figure that you don't belong to him, that you belong to God. Another time, he told me of a visit he had just had from a more fundamentalist pastor who—knowing that he had AIDS—announced authoritatively that he was going to hell if he didn't repent of his sins, presumably to this pastor. I hit the ceiling, then complained to the hospital authorities, who were as outraged by this invasion of the young man's room as I was. But the patient was able to take it all with equanimity.

One of my most moving pastoral experiences came when this same young man lay dying in a suburban Maryland hospital. On his last day on earth, with life ebbing away, his mother was with him for support. She was a longtime member of a fundamentalist church in another state. Her pastor there was harsh in his judgment of her son. I am not aware that she felt the full effect of her church's moralistic theology, but it did not matter. Hour after hour, she sat by her son's bedside, cradling his head in her arms, bathing his fevered forehead with a cool cloth, speaking quietly and tenderly. I do not know that I have ever witnessed as pure an expression of the grace of God as I did in that hospital room. And it was also a needed reminder that there are times when it is possible for people to rise above their narrow theological principles into the realm of God's grace. She was certainly an inspiration to me.

Everybody's life is precious, but some deaths receive more attention than others. A death in one of our church families was destined to receive a good deal of national publicity. Early one morning in 1994 the phone rang. It was former senator and presidential candidate George McGovern, a Foundry member. He was obviously heartbroken. The body of his daughter Terry, age forty-five, had just been discovered, frozen, on a snowbank in Madison, Wisconsin. Terry had had a serious alcohol problem. She had been in and out of various rehabilitation centers, and she had been involved in twelve-step programs such as Alcoholics Anonymous. At times she appeared to have recovered. Most AA members will tell you that you never fully recover from alcoholism, but many have been able to stay dry for the rest of their lives. Terry was one of those who could not. Despite her addiction, her family and friends knew her as highly intelligent and warmly caring. After her death, in fact, several people came forward to say how much she had helped *them* to conquer the addiction. At her funeral service, one of these people spoke eloquently of how she had saved his life by encouraging him in his battle against the demons of alcoholism. But her own death had come when she had, once again, had too much to drink one bitterly cold night, passed out on the snowbank, and not been discovered until morning.

Senator McGovern wrote a best-selling book about the tragedy and what had led up to it and about the severities of the disease of alcoholism.[1] He was brutally honest about his own self-perceived failings as a parent. My own pastoral impression is that he was far too hard on himself. Most parents end up feeling they haven't been able to devote enough time to their children. Where there are tragedies like Terry's, there are enough other factors at work to make us pause before judging (such as the wider cultural climate during the times when a child is growing up and, in the case of alcoholism, some specific physiological factors). In Terry's case, her intellectual capabilities and her warm, self-giving nature also speak volumes about parents who helped cultivate such gifts in her formative years.

In a church of Foundry's size and location, one might expect a certain number of accidental and suicidal deaths during a ten-year period. None

1. George McGovern, *Terry* (New York: Villard, 1996).

of our members died by suicide during my years there, though if any had I would not have been judgmental about that either.

The Young, The Old

A tragic accidental death snuffed out the life of a very promising young man in the church before he reached the age of thirty. Adam Darling was a political appointee who had served mainly in the Commerce Department. He was so well thought of by Secretary of Commerce Ron Brown that Brown asked him to come along on a trade negotiation trip to the Balkans. Adam was on Secretary Brown's plane when it crashed in Croatia in 1996, killing all on board. I hadn't known Adam well, but I was to learn more after his death. He was one of a large number of young adults in our church and had chosen to live in inner-city Washington out of his commitment to the city. He had helped energize a whole neighborhood, and he was remembered fondly by the children with whom he played outdoor games. Everybody liked him. At his parents' request, I flew out to their home in Santa Cruz, California, to preach in Adam's funeral service. (Hillary Clinton, also in California at the time, came to the service and spoke warmly of the admiration she and the president had for this young man.) A few days later we held a memorial service at Foundry for Adam's many Washington friends.

Most of the other deaths in our church were of people who weren't that young. But in 1993, death came out of the blue to the twenty-three-year-old son of a Foundry member who had originally come to this country from Jamaica. This young man, a recent college graduate, was beginning a teaching career in Iowa. He became ill, complications developed and spun out of control, and suddenly he was gone. His mother, a devout Christian who loved this son very much, taught me a lesson or two about grace in the presence of tragedy. Loss of a son or daughter can be an almost unbearable sorrow, and her grief was real. Still, her faith was unwavering and her love for everybody was compelling. Pastors are supposed to be channels of God's grace in such situations, but often it is the faith and love of parishioners that helps us find the inner resources to minister.

The youngest person to die on my watch was the two-month-old son of a bright young couple in the church. They had married at Foundry. They dearly wanted to have a child. When complications developed in the pregnancy, the expectant mother willingly endured a couple of months in a hospital bed to facilitate a safe delivery. But the baby was born prematurely, and despite the best efforts of excellent physicians, everything that could go wrong did go wrong. We held a moving service of baptism for the little fellow at Children's Hospital of Washington shortly before his death. The gathered family, there to support the couple and to join in mourning, reminded me once again of the deeply communal nature of all life and of how we can all be bound more deeply to one another in a shared faith in God's enduring care. (I'm pleased to note, as a postscript, that the grieving parents had a very healthy baby boy the next year, this time without complications.)

Naturally, our response to death is different when it comes at the end of a very long, productive life. I was surprised to discover at the end of my Foundry tenure that I had had funerals or memorial services for nineteen people in their nineties. Each was unique, of course. In most cases, death came as conclusion to life fully lived.

We all loved and appreciated Genevieve Taylor, the church treasurer I referred to in chapter 2. Genevieve had been a part of Foundry since before World War II. While single herself, she had participated through the church school in the rearing of generations of three-year-olds. Amazingly, she had taught the three-year-old Sunday School class for more than fifty continuous years. During the 1940s, she had had a bout of breast cancer from which she had recovered, but in her late eighties cancer struck again. She was a courageous as well as kindly woman, but she was clearly troubled as she began a round of chemotherapy. It wasn't because of discomfort or fear of death, she said. It was that she was almost certain to lose her hair. "Now Genevieve," I remonstrated with her. "What are you saying to me?" I asked as I ran my hand over my bald head. "Oh," she laughed. "That's different. You're a man." We almost lost Genevieve during the months that followed, but she rallied and came back for another year or so before death claimed her at age ninety-one—with, by that time, a full head of hair.

Death also came at age ninety-one to the venerable Dr. Arthur Flemming. He had been president of three universities, a member of President Eisenhower's cabinet, and, until fired by President Reagan, chair of the U.S. Civil Rights Commission. Moving into his nineties, Arthur just kept going and was not about to "go gentle into that good night," nor was he particularly afraid of death. It was just, he said, that he had so many things to do! When I came to know him, well into his late eighties, Arthur was still maintaining an extraordinary schedule of speaking around the country and supervising a variety of organizations his creative mind had spawned to do all kinds of good works for humanity. I still cherish the lunch sessions I had, at his invitation, for an updating on the state of the church, the world, and his various concerns. Often he would treat me to a living history lesson as he reminisced on his relationships with nearly every U.S. president since Calvin Coolidge.

Only toward the end of his life did I learn that Arthur had suffered from diabetes for decades. As his wife, Bernice, observed, he had learned to "conform to the discipline of his disease." He had become living proof that diabetes is not necessarily a killer, not even in great age. But Arthur suffered a fall and a broken hip in August 1996. Even that didn't stop him at first. Once, visiting him in hospital, I asked whether this was crimping his style. "Not at all," he grinned. "As long as I have this [he pointed to the bedside telephone], I'm in business." He observed that in his ninety-one years this was his very first time to be a patient in a hospital.

But it was also the last time. Complications set in. Kidney failure ensued. Dialysis was not a possibility. I don't think he expected to die until about two days before the end, and then he took it with great grace. By then he had been returned to the health care unit of his retirement home, and nothing further could be done for him medically. He was unconscious most of his last day. That evening I called on him, and the family encouraged me to try to rouse him. So I went in and spoke, "Arthur." Opening a bleary eye toward me, he said, "Hi, Phil." I asked if he would like to have Communion, and he said he would. I mentally kicked myself for having forgotten to bring along the handy little Communion kit most ministers pack around. So I recruited family members to look for bread and grape juice or wine in other parts of the building. The bread was no problem, of course, but they couldn't seem to locate grape juice or wine anywhere. The best anybody could come up with was grapefruit juice. So Arthur Flemming's last Communion was with bread and grapefruit juice. At least the word *grape* was involved, and I'm confident that our Lord was not in the least offended.

Consolation and Celebration

Many pastors dread having to do funerals. I can understand why. Sometimes we don't know exactly what to say as we meet with bereaved loved ones. There are certain conventions about such times, but there can also be a note of unreality. Sometimes that is so if the service is in a mortuary setting rather than a church. The problem is how to help people face the reality of death, but in such a way that grace abounds and there can be deep healing.

I didn't want those moments to come. When they did come, it was often to people I had come to know and love, and I too was going to miss them. There is also a touch of awkwardness as we approach what is bound to be a very crucial time in the lives of those who have lost somebody dear, and we don't feel ready for it. Still, something somehow does take hold of us. The very sense that this is such an important time in the lives of these people can be energizing. There descends a certain realization that this also is an important time for us. I don't believe I ever took ministry to the bereaved in a casual or purely routine way, but as the years went by, the sense of its importance increased.

At the same time, I came to realize when I sat down with a sorrowing family that the particular words didn't matter nearly as much as the spirit, the friendly support, even the mere fact of being present. One doesn't have to *talk* all that much! Better to listen and then find caring words and words of faith. Prayer under those conditions can come quite spontaneously, sometimes from the vast resources of Christian tradition.

In planning for the memorial service or funeral (the distinction is that the corpse is present at a funeral), often done together with the family or closest friends, a good pastor respects their wishes. This probably is not the time to tamper with people's musical taste, for instance. In a handful of cases I found I had to be a bit of a diplomat, mediating differences between family members whose conflicts obviously didn't begin with this death. Sometimes it has seemed advisable to steer people gently in one direction or another for the sake of what they themselves would ultimately get out of the service.

I regularly used and like the United Methodist service of death and resurrection. One would never use all of it since there are options built into the flow of the liturgy. But I find most of the language helpful, and there is a nice progression from beginning to end. I usually asked the survivors whether the deceased had any favorite passages from Scripture and any favorite hymns. Sometimes there would be a clear answer, but more often than not the family simply would not know. Using a metaphor derived from the computer age, I sometimes told the family or friends that if they didn't have any particular preferences there would be a kind of "default drive" that would work out the details without their having to worry about them. A majority of our services at Foundry were in the church itself, most often in the main sanctuary. I believe that a church setting is often much to be preferred for several reasons: It is a place that usually was familiar to the deceased in life. It is a place where worship occurs, and a memorial service or funeral is above all else an act of worship. There is less strangeness or artificiality about it—or so it has seemed to me. A majority of services at Foundry were also memorial services. Most, but certainly not all, families chose cremation rather than a coffin burial.

Typically, Walt Shropshire and I did the services together. He would take primary responsibility for the early part of the service, except for a word of greeting from me. I would do the New Testament reading and a short sermon. He would then go through the congregation with a handheld microphone, inviting anybody to say a few words of appreciation and remembrance. (Sometimes families were afraid this would get out of hand, but Walt was very good at setting this up, making people comfortable, and drawing it to an appropriate ending when it was time.) I would then conclude the service with prayers of commendation and thanksgiving and a benediction. Eileen Guenther, if available (as she generally was), would work out the music beautifully.

Every service was unique because every individual is unique. After a year or so, I began to realize that there is an almost mysterious way in which death brings the threads of a person's life into focus. It often is possible to discern a certain note about that person, for in death the meaning of a person's life seems to be more easily defined. I don't want to overstate this, but in conversation with those who were closest to the deceased, I often heard the same things over and over. In preparation for my own brief sermon, I would look for that unifying note and great passages of Scripture that might best capture it. I discovered that the eighth chapter of Paul's letter to the Romans was often the richest seedbed of insight. Here we have an utter frankness about the futility of existence—not that earthly life is meaningless but that it all comes to an end—and even the reminder that the whole creation is subject to decay. Those words can be comforting, oddly enough, to the family of somebody who has deteriorated mentally and physically beyond recognition, but they must be accompanied by the great message of hope running through Romans 8, with its eloquent conclusion that nothing can separate us from the love of God.

I would usually recall a few particulars about a person's life, anticipating the longer period when Walt's roving microphone would pick up additional information and words of appreciation. There would often be space for some humor, both in my sermon and in the period of witness by others. Indeed, one of the striking things about a real service of death and resurrection is how faith, grief, and humor can be blended. Such a service is almost bound to be a time of emotion, and these emotions are wide ranging. I never spoke words of condemnation, nor used the service as an evangelistic tool. (I am intrigued by the fact that people who had been away from churches for years were attracted to Foundry on a more permanent basis by a funeral; thus, sometimes the service served an evangelistic function indirectly.) Once in a long while something negative might be said by somebody during the witness period, though usually as preface to a word of praise. I still chuckle over one such witness. The setting was a service, attended by a large number of people, for a well-known figure in various social causes. He wasn't a Foundry member—I don't even know whether he had ever attended our church—but because of a number of other associations and a specific request, we did the service. While he was much admired, he had had a somewhat thorny personality, around which most of the witnesses skated successfully. But one spokesperson got right to the point: "We all know," he announced from the lectern, "that [name withheld] was the meanest son of a bitch in Washington." The crowd laughed uproariously. But everybody also nodded appreciatively when the spokesperson continued, commending social justice commitments and accomplishments of the deceased and his personal affection for this colorful man.

Our services involved people of high visibility and prestige and people of very low social standing. Sometimes, as in the instance I just mentioned, there would be a very large congregation; sometimes but a handful of people. Still, the overall impression I have from scores of services through the years is that these are "leveling" moments. Many things that seem to matter most in life matter scarcely at all in death. In the end we shall be quickly forgotten; our hope is in God who is not impressed, I'm sure, by most of our human distinctions. Ministry to a diverse congregation like Foundry can bring to mind the words of Gray's "Elegy Written in a Country Churchyard":

> Let not Ambition mock their useful toil,
> Their homely joys, and destiny obscure;
> Nor Grandeur hear with a disdainful smile
> The short and simple annals of the poor.

Gray's further observation that "the paths of glory lead but to the grave" is not the whole story, but it may be the part of the story most to be remembered in this city.

How Healing Comes

Much has been written and said about healing and "closure." The longer I served as pastor the more complicated that seemed to me. For some people, the acceptance of impending death has seemed easy, but for others this time is excruciatingly fearful and difficult. There is wisdom in

Elisabeth Kübler-Ross's famous delineation of stages of preparation for death—although death is certainly going to come to us whether we are ready or not, and our psychological state at the time of death may be less important than some suppose. That point aside, I have seen terminally ill persons for whom the brief months or years became a gift of love in the way in which they were lived—and I have seen people for whom it wasn't quite so easy. One doctor who often treated terminally ill patients remarked that people tend to die about as they lived. The process of dying tends, he observed, to bring out who we really are. I'm not sure I want to believe that in quite such stark terms, mostly I suppose because I've seen people who didn't die very well, and I don't want to define their whole lives by that fact. Still, it is a part of the pastoral task to help those who are dying to be the very best that they can be.

If people vary in their ability to handle their own impending death, it is also true that survivors vary in the time it takes to find healing. I know that was true in my own case. The sudden death of my father was harder to adjust to than the death of my mother following a long, painful, terminal illness, maybe because I was older when my father died, and we had been able to forge an adult relationship. Or maybe it was because the grief work had, in the case of my mother, been accomplished more in the months before her death and thus was not as large a preoccupation after she was gone. I simply do not know. I do know from my pastoral experience that the process varies with people. In several instances elderly widows or widowers have said months or even years later how much they continue to miss their spouses. I've seen very few instances of the kind of morbid attachments that can dominate a person's life for many years, but it strikes me as normal, and not at all morbid, to continue to miss someone who has been such an important part of one's life.

How then does healing come? With some it is by forging new relationships, especially by finding new persons (not necessarily new spouses) in whom to invest the gift of loving service. With some there can come a deeper sense of the continued presence of a loved one who has died, again not morbidly but somewhat in the manner in which even great persons of past generations can continue to be a living presence.

I do not doubt that for most people the continuing support of a caring community like a church can make all the difference. And thus I have witnessed with growing appreciation how the special gift of a church like Foundry can bring healing to people.

Chapter Six

Preaching to Both Heart and Mind

In which I seek to put my years of studying and teaching Christian ethics into practice in the pulpit—deepen my understanding of what "prophetic" preaching means—decide which public issues to take on—confront and learn from criticism—reflect on the well-publicized departure of a well-known parishioner

When I had nearly completed my Foundry journey, a church leader remarked to me that she had had some apprehensions at the beginning. In a nice letter to me she put it this way: "Having spent my working life in higher education I've become accustomed to poking fun at faculty. So, I said to myself, hmmm, I wonder if this academic guy can engage in applied Christianity." Sometimes I'd wondered about that myself, so I suspect she wasn't the only member of Foundry who had such questions. Her question had to do with practical aspects of ministry, including pastoral service, administration, and social action. She couldn't have known about the practical matters I had engaged in during the years, but her question—and the congregation's—probably also had to do with whether I could focus all these various components to preaching.

I have always known that preaching is not the same thing as lecturing, and yet sermons are not intended just to make people feel good. They must have intellectual content as well as emotional appeal. The question is how to preach to the heart and the mind at the same time.

Addressing Social Issues

For me, social issues were no small matter. I had spent twenty-six years in a seminary classroom, trying to persuade generations of future preachers to include the mind along with the heart. Since my field was Christian ethics, that meant encouraging students to relate their faith to social as well as personal issues. I could not turn my back on all that teaching now that I was myself preaching regularly. It was time to put up or shut up! So, from the beginning, I spoke to the issues of the day from the pulpit—and also to problems that needed to become issues of the day.

On the whole, the congregation was very receptive, but there were exceptions. One person, obviously struggling with a host of personal issues, pleaded with me to devote greater emphasis to the spiritual problems of the people. People are dying out there, she wrote me with urgency. Reading between the lines, I realized that she felt I was too detached in my intellectual world to perceive the spiritual wounds of many. Maybe she was right. It did take me a while to sense the depth of the brokenness of numbers of people in the congregation and to respond with pastoral sensitivity. Nevertheless, I could not divorce the needs of persons from the brokenness of the world in which we all have to live. Nor could I separate the mind from the heart by speaking only to how we feel and not to how we think.

The problem presents itself most directly when people resist preaching that deals with very specific issues. I was reminded of that unforgettably when I received a letter in late May 1994. The previous Sunday I had preached a "peace with justice" sermon, with Isaiah 32:16–18 as the principal text. The sermon dealt broadly with the dilemma Christians have always faced in relating love to military force. I quoted Jacques Ellul to illustrate the pacifist position, but then identified my own thinking more with a passage from Karl Barth in which that theologian pays tribute to pacifism but ultimately rejects its sweeping dismissal of all force. I went on to speak of violence and injustice (including even genocide) in places such as Bosnia, Rwanda, and Haiti. "How are we to deal with such challenges?" I asked. The answer, I proposed: "Power must be employed in such a world with great wisdom and restraint. I do not think we have the luxury of turning aside because we fear the cost of responding effectively. . . . I cannot think of anything more threatening to the national interest than a world in which anarchy, and flagrant disregard for human rights, and human wretchedness are allowed to progress unchecked."

A day or so later, the letter arrived. "Regarding the sermon last Sunday," the writer commented, "I for one felt that there were several 'presidential policy options' embedded in the latter part of your remarks, and I think it is preferable to avoid such specific recommendations when you have 'the most prominent parishioner' caught in the congregation." The writer was clearly referring to President Clinton's presence, which had, I thought, been entirely uncoerced! The writer concluded that "the earlier part of the sermon, when dealing with the exegesis of Isaiah and the theology of Barth, was interesting and sufficiently remote from the current choices facing the country."

In fairness to the author of the letter, whom I came to know later, there certainly are some homileticians who believe that it is better to keep our moral teachings general and allow people to frame the specifics in their own minds. A good sermon will often do some of that. But aren't the implications of the last line of the letter fascinating? The part of the sermon that could be approved was the section that was "sufficiently remote from the current choices facing the country." If that were adopted as a guideline for all preaching it would certainly have to apply to times other than when the president of the United States is in attendance, as well. A sermon would have to remain "sufficiently remote" from all kinds of choices currently facing all kinds of people! A certain amount of specificity seems necessary to illustrate the generalities and also to make clear that our faith really does speak to the issues we are actually facing.

Of course, the preacher cannot pretend to have all the answers. We are not infallible; we can be wrong. The more specific we get—especially on controversial issues—the greater our responsibility to acknowledge our limitations. We can frankly say that we could be wrong. That, in my opinion, doesn't weaken the force of our message. It can even strengthen it by emphasizing the honesty of the pulpit and the depth of our commitment to truth. It can also show respect for the thinking of others in the congregation.

Since the format of a worship service rarely, if ever, allows people to voice their disagreements, it is well to structure later "talk-back" sessions. One of the most interesting of those at Foundry occurred during the summer of 1994. The administration's task force on health care, chaired by Hillary Clinton, had proposed sweeping changes in the nation's health care delivery system that were designed to ensure health care for all. I had some reservations about the proposal, largely because I believed the changes should have been *more* sweeping! The task force's proposals left a role for existing health care plans and insurance carriers; I was more persuaded by the wisdom of a single-payer system, perhaps modeled on Canadian if not British experience. Politically, I could understand why the Clintons had stopped short of that. The major campaign against their proposals, heavily funded by the health care insurers themselves, was from those who felt they went too far. In any event, I considered this an issue that had to be addressed from the pulpit. I argued that health care for all has the strongest support in our faith, and that we should be clear about that basic goal. The specific program chosen to achieve the goal might be more debatable. But of the actual, achievable possibilities, I felt I could support the Clinton proposals. Still, I observed that there was room for debate. I announced the week before preaching on the issue that I was going to do so and that we would schedule a discussion session immediately following in the sanctuary. Since the congregation included a number of congressional staffers and others who were very knowledgeable on the subject, it proved to be an extraordinary session. I wouldn't have missed it for anything. Among the most helpful comments were those of Arthur Flemming, a stronger supporter of the Clinton plan who had a wealth of experience with such issues at the national level.

In hindsight, I realize I didn't arrange this kind of discussion often enough. That was partly in recognition that, unless the subject is really a hotly contested one, attendance often isn't all that great. Nevertheless, it is an acknowledgment that (as a perceptive slogan puts it) "none of us is wiser than all of us put together."

Most Foundry people appreciated having a preacher who engaged the issues. Some even went out of their way to tell me that that is what attracted them to the church in the first place—but not everybody. During the early years, several people sought me out to express feelings a little like those of the letter writer I mentioned earlier, often to object to the injection of "politics" in sermons. I myself have strong reservations about taking partisan political positions in sermons if that means favoring one candidate or party over another in elections.[1] While I have generally voted for Democratic candidates, I made it a point during my Foundry years not to give public electoral endorsements even outside the pulpit. When people voiced opposition to "politics" in the pulpit, they generally referred to the discussion of public policy issues. Sometimes the objections seemed motivated by the positions I had taken: I was on the wrong "side." More typically, however, the critics had a very different conception of what preaching is all about. As one person put it to me, worship is the one time in the week when she can get some relief from having to deal with issues. Worship was seen by this member as a kind of island of peace in the midst of a week of conflict. I can understand that. Yet what is the point of the island if it doesn't help us deal with the conflicts and tensions of the real

1. I have discussed my reasons for that more fully in my book, *Christian Perspectives on Politics*, rev. and expanded ed. (Louisville, Ky.: Westminster John Knox Press, 2000).

world? Worship should help us get the rest of life in focus so that the island of peace becomes, in a manner of speaking, the whole continent.

With the rising influence of right-wing Christian political groups during the 1990s—exemplified especially by the Christian Coalition—I sometimes joked that that movement (with which I disagreed about many things) had almost persuaded me that Christians should avoid *all* involvements with politics. Yet my quarrel with those brothers and sisters in the faith was less with form and more with substance. On those occasions when I've heard the sermons of others at a time of national crisis or controversy, I have been more offended by irrelevancy than by what I considered wrongheadedness. I recall one sermon by a fellow pastor during the Gulf War of 1991 that was, I thought, mistaken in its conclusions. He was specifically respectful of those who disagreed, but equally forthright in expressing the conclusions to which he had been led. I respected that. In no way did it interfere with my worship experience; it enhanced it. Subsequently, I heard a sermon in a military chapel, by a chaplain, that ignored the war altogether. I probably would have agreed with the chaplain's view, assuming he supported the war, but we'll never know about that! Frankly, I was more offended by his silence. It left the impression that the God we worship on Sunday has nothing to do with the realities of the world we face the rest of the week.

That, I am confident, was not the view of most Foundry people—but, again, not all. Several singled me out for lengthy conferences in my office, which I was happy to arrange. One launched a campaign of sorts with the Staff-Parish Relations Committee, seeking leverage to get me to change or (perhaps) be removed. A handful of members, including this person, withdrew from the church. My impression, however, is that many more were attracted to the church because of its willingness to address issues. Even if that had not been the case, I do not think I could have turned away from what I have always considered to be a fundamental task of the pulpit. I especially appreciated the loyalty to the church shown by those who continued to feel that public issues should not be injected into sermons but who stayed with the church in spite of their disagreements. Maybe we all learned something from one another.

After I had been at Foundry for several years, one Sunday Carolyn and I were on the West Coast and attended services at the famous Glide Memorial United Methodist Church in San Francisco. That church, located in the heart of the city, is known for its inclusiveness, its prophetic message to the arenas of public life, and its wide-ranging efforts to serve the homeless and AIDS victims. In many respects, Glide was a reflection of its dynamic leader of many years, the Rev. Cecil Williams. When we attended Glide, Rev. Williams was preaching. I sat bolt upright in my pew when he said, "I know many of you don't like to hear about politics from the pulpit, but . . ." and went on to explain why it is necessary to address public issues in preaching. Well, said I to myself, who am I to complain about those who criticize my addressing such issues if Cecil Williams, after thirty years in a church largely built around his charismatic personality, still finds it necessary to so preface his political remarks from the pulpit!

Choosing Issues—and Paying a Price

Obviously a pastor cannot speak to every issue that comes along. To be effective, one must be selective. I'm sure I'm not the best judge of which issues I addressed most effectively. I imagine that different members of the congregation would judge that differently. I know I *felt* most effective when the problem at hand involved marginalized or vulnerable people whose plight needed to be illuminated in light of Christian faith, love, and justice. My whole upbringing had contributed to that. When I was only eleven years old, our family moved from Ohio to Arizona for my father's health. There, in tiny Somerton, we experienced great racial and ethnic diversity and a well-demarcated social hierarchy. My father's small church served the top of the social ladder, but both my father and mother were deeply committed to an inclusive society in which all are accepted and respected. It must have rubbed off. I embarrassed my parents a bit when I stood and challenged a racist teacher in my seventh-grade classroom. My parents suggested better ways of approaching such a situation, but their criticism was mild to say the least. In that small Yuma Valley community the migrant workers, the kinds of people John Steinbeck immortalized in his *Grapes of Wrath*, were among the most marginalized. I devoted considerable energy later in graduate school to migrant workers and, as a professor myself, I sought to gain student support for the farm workers movement of Cesar Chavez. I was similarly involved through the years in the civil rights movement. I didn't take on such things for the sake of political correctness, but for the sake of people.

Nothing in my Foundry experience led me to change these basic attitudes. Nevertheless, I came to understand better how the Christian gospel relates to vulnerable people. In particular, I recall now the deeper insight I gained through preparation of one specific sermon, part of a Lenten series on "The Way of the Cross," which I preached in 1997. Each sermon explored some aspect of what it means to share the life of Christ on the cross—as in "Sharing the Pain," "Sharing the Love," "Sharing the Sorrow." The particular sermon that stands out in my recollection now was "Sharing the Stigma." In some branches of Christianity much is made of the *stigmata*, the marks of the nails and spear on the body of Christ that some mystics claim to have appeared on their own bodies. My sermon was not about that tradition; instead, it was about how Christ was willing to be identified with socially stigmatized people—the outcasts, sinners, tax collectors, the hated Samaritans, and so forth. As I wrestled with this theme it became evident to me that Jesus' willingness to befriend such people was at the very heart of his ministry. Perhaps it was a central, if not *the* most important reason for his crucifixion. To share the stigma of rejected people is, I said in my sermon, to invite being rejected oneself. Whether or not that happens, Christian life is not fully authentic if it goes along with popular prejudices. I believe that preaching on the situation of marginalized people can contribute greatly to the authenticity of the whole worship experience.

I have also given high priority to major events currently gripping the consciousness of the nation, especially as these illustrate broader issues—the Oklahoma City disaster, the events of September 11, times of national elections, the presidential crisis of 1998–99. Such events invite religious interpretation. We can be wrong in our interpretation, of course, but we cannot ignore them. Even a faulty interpretation can, by raising the subject, invite thoughtful response and an improved perspective.

One word of caution: It can be tempting for a preacher who is attached to some particular issue to ride it to death. I tried to avoid that, although I am sure there were people at Foundry who felt I said too much about some subjects and maybe not enough about others.

I had to face an unusual test myself on two Sundays in late 1994. I had planned a sermon series for Advent on what Christians hope for. One of these was to be on our hope to be included; another was on our hope for peace. Both resonated to the biblical texts usually central to Advent services. In the first of these, I spoke of what it means to be excluded. Most of us don't really know, although we may have an occasional sense of that when we are slighted or not included in some social occasion. But, I continued, it can be very different if you are of a racial minority, or gay, or a welfare recipient (here I quoted from a marvelous passage in Russell Baker's *Growing Up*, in which he wrote of his family's humiliation at having to receive public assistance during the Depression). Looking out on the congregation that morning I spotted Senator Robert Dole, about to become Senate majority leader. I had gotten to know Senator and Mrs.

Dole in my two years at Foundry. We had a friendly relationship, but other commitments precluded his church attendance except on rare occasions. But here he was, as I was about to preach. A couple of points in the sermon were likely to be at cross-purposes with his political views, but I made no changes. The senator greeted me affably at the door, and I assumed I wouldn't be seeing him again for a few months.

Then, two weeks later, the sermon topic was our hope for peace. This sermon, also grounded in Advent texts, got specific about the world situation. The U.S. intervention in Haiti was still in the news. While recognizing ambiguities in that situation, I wanted to support that effort by the United States to bring an end to out-and-out tyranny in our Caribbean neighbor. President Clinton was at the first service and, later in the day, he thanked me for that public support of the way he had addressed a difficult dilemma. As I looked out on the congregation before commencing the second service, whom should I see but Senator Dole. The senator had publicly and vigorously opposed the Haiti intervention. So, was I to contest his views from the pulpit on two out of three Sundays?

As I explained the situation to a friend later, it was as though Satan himself had perched on my shoulder and said, "Are you sure you want to go through with the Haiti part of your sermon?" I reflected on the matter for a few moments before saying, "Get thee behind me, Satan! The very fact that you have raised the question with me is all the more reason why I should proceed as though the senator were not present." While I should add that I don't believe in the existence of Satan as a literal being, I certainly do believe in his functional equivalents—as illustrated in this little situation and countless others when we are tempted to turn away from what we believe to be right and good.

Senator Dole voiced no criticism to me personally following the service, but as a matter of fact this turned out to be the last time I saw him in church. After a period of "church shopping," he and his wife formed a relationship with a church of another denomination. I honestly don't believe the reason for their departure from Foundry was those sermons or any others, even though it was put out in the press that they had left because they found the minister to be too liberal. Maybe so. But I think there were larger reasons. Senator Dole was about to run for the Republican nomination for president. He might have found it awkward to be in the same church as his Democratic opponent, President Clinton. For the two leading candidates for president to be a part of the same church could have been a wonderful example to the nation, and I would indeed have done nothing during such a campaign to show a partisan preference. But

I can see why the senator might have found it awkward. The Christian Coalition was enormously influential in the Republican Party at that time. Senator Dole, while not their first choice (and probably not sharing many of their views), doubtless had to at least be acceptable to them, and Foundry Church had already been singled out for attack by that movement (as I explain in chapter 11). The senator may have been prompted partly by such political considerations.

Trying to Get It Right

Of course, it isn't enough to be bold and prophetic. A pastor also has a responsibility, so far as possible, to be wise. How are we to discern the will of God in the face of monumental uncertainties and conflicting voices?

Some issues seem very clear. Among serious Christians there is no longer any doubt that slavery is an evil and that racism and racial discrimination are flatly wrong. There is a broad consensus among most Christians in support of religious liberty, although there remain some differences regarding detail. American Christians, in common with Christians of many countries, can be counted in support of democratic political institutions. Many Protestants, including most of my fellow United Methodists, believe in full equality for women, including now the right of women to be ordained. The degree of consensus at a recent United Methodist General Conference in opposition to the death penalty was surprisingly high. It can be possible simply to accept the thorough discernment process that has brought the church to deeply held agreement, although it must be added immediately that some widely and deeply held agreements have proved to be wrong. As James Russell Lowell's poem puts it, "Time makes ancient good uncouth"—at least sometimes it does.

But it remains that Christians of every era have to face dilemmas and quandaries and uncertainties. In our time, abortion and homosexuality remain deeply divisive issues. New findings in the biological sciences, such as the possibilities of stem cell research and cloning, are confusing to many, myself included. The emergence of a "new world order" in law, politics, and economics is not yet fully thought through (the phrase originated, by the way, with American Christians during World War II in anticipation of the postwar world). American Christians are perplexed about the role and responsibilities of their country as the world's remaining superpower. People the world over are deeply affected by decisions made here, and they rightly want to share in the decision making. How to discern the implications of the faith in such a world? The pulpit, again, cannot pretend to have all the answers. But it would be irresponsible not to struggle with the issues in preaching.

Part of my stock-in-trade as a Christian ethicist had been the development of a method of moral judgment based on clarification of our initial presumptions. If we can gain clarity about the starting point, we at least know where to place the burden of proof. The classical "just war" doctrine illustrates this. The presumption of Christians, according to that teaching, is that war is a great evil that should never be entered into lightly or routinely. The Christian's initial presumption should always be against war. But, according to the doctrine, there may be situations of oppression or aggression that are an even greater evil. In such cases the burden of proof should be against war, not for it. The seven or so criteria of just war doctrine are designed as tests to determine when the burden of proof has been met. Many thoughtful Christians concluded that American entry into World War II met the test; some, like Reinhold Niebuhr, reached that conclusion even before the attack on Pearl Harbor. On the other hand, many Christians (again including Niebuhr) believed that the Vietnam War did not meet the moral standard.

That kind of approach has broad applicability in other areas where we face moral uncertainties, but it requires thought. Sometimes, even in the pulpit, it is possible to engage a congregation using that kind of format. As one illustration, late in my ministry at Foundry, I became excited with the possibilities of a global school lunch program that Ambassador George McGovern had proposed in his role as ambassador to the United Nations Food and Agriculture agencies in Rome. The UN became enthusiastic about this idea when it was shown to involve costs of less than $10 billion per year. I related that proposal to the deeply Christian commitment to feed the poor. The presumption of Christians is that we must do whatever we can. As I asked in the sermon, why don't we just *do* it? The burden of proof would have to be borne by opposition to such an attractive proposal. A number of complicating problems can be posed, none of them sufficient in my judgment to oppose the idea. (I had explored this at length with Ambassador McGovern himself while visiting him at his post in Rome in 2000, and with several diplomats of other nations and the UN.) We have a responsibility as Christians to work out the problems and get on with feeding the children.[2]

2. I was delighted to learn that Ambassador McGovern had been joined by former Senator Dole in presenting this idea to President Clinton, who used his budgetary discretion to put some $300 million in a number of pilot projects.

As I felt my way into the task of preaching regularly to the same congregation, I found I was doing less topical preaching than I had expected. A topical sermon is one that is addressed to a single issue, attempting to explore it thoroughly and relating it, of course, to the shared faith. My predecessor had preached such a sermon, memorably and courageously, on the subject of homosexuality some years before my arrival, and I have benefited by hearing and reading other such efforts on a variety of topics. At one time or another I attempted sermons in which I sought to illuminate a whole "landscape": What is the meaning of politics? What is the meaning of economics? What should be a broad Christian perspective on such spheres? In effect, you could say such a sermon is about how Christians should relate to ideologies, although that is very far from substituting ideology for faith. For instance, solid theological reasons can be given in support of democracy, but that is very far from making democracy the object of worship. It is even farther from treating the American version as a perfect example of what democracy ought to be. I had studied and written extensively on such broad issues before going to Foundry. There was, I thought, a place for sharing this from the pulpit.

Still, such efforts were infrequent. On the whole, I found it much more useful to touch on social issues as a part of the development of a sermon based on a biblical-theological theme. I was surprised to discover how easily and naturally that could be done. Sometimes, when tempted to change an announced sermon topic in light of a major development in the world, I discovered I could deal with the current issue as a part of what I had already planned. One illustration of that was a post-Easter sermon at the time of the Oklahoma City bombing. The sermon, from Psalm 30:11, was to be "From Mourning to Dancing." At first glance, that joyous Easter theme seemed crudely insensitive to the enormity of the tragedy. But Easter itself was born out of tragedy; in the end, the announced topic was better than I could have managed with any substitute. I did change sermon subjects on a handful of occasions—such as when the church was plunged into crisis my first year, the big snow Sunday of 1993, and the Sunday following the disaster of September 11, 2001.

I generally made it a practice to look over the Sunday morning newspaper before leaving for church. Now and then there would be some item that fit in, and mentioning this reminded the congregation that our faith relates directly to the ongoing flow of our life together in the world. Thus, for instance, I could speak to the assassination of Prime Minister Rabin of Israel. Those times when I missed a major event the sermon was the worse for it.

A Prophetic Pulpit

Preaching on social issues is sometimes referred to as *prophetic.* Sometimes I think preachers themselves think of *prophetic* as necessarily meaning controversial and maybe involving raising one's voice a bit more than usual. Well, not so fast.

The word itself originates in a Greek term for somebody who is a spokesperson for somebody else. In the time-honored tradition of Jews and Christians, a *prophet* is one who speaks for God. Sometimes that entails being controversial, even a bit contentious. But while the word of God is not always controversial, it is always profound, always out of the depths. That can even mean a deep word of comfort, as in the magnificent message of Isaiah 40 that was addressed to a thoroughly beaten people in their Babylonian exile. I would consider a message of encouragement and affirmation to people who have given up on themselves to be prophetic. And even when the message must be controversial, it is for the sake of the spiritual wholeness of those who are being confronted as well as those whom they are oppressing. Racists need to hear a confronting word, not just for the sake of those whom they despise but for the sake of their own salvation—the restoration of their loving relationship with God and with all of God's children. Persons abusing their spouses need to confront their spiritual brokenness, just as those being abused need to find comfort and new strength to change their life situation.

On the basis of this understanding of the prophetic, I am disinclined to draw a line between preaching on social issues and other matters that properly claim the pulpit's attention.

Roman Catholic theologians have long understood that the church's teaching extends from the deepest faith commitments (or dogmas) to the most specific applications, with various doctrines arranged in between. The more specific the applications, the more contingent they are upon different situations and changing insights. Often the church must speak with greater tentativeness, the more specific its address to the factual world. But no line should be drawn between basic faith and application. To neglect either is to call the faith into question. The deeper I got into my ministry at Foundry, the more I found myself needing to address very basic faith questions.

Chapter Seven

Faith Questions

In which I discover how deep the questions people of our times have about matters of belief—why serious doubt can be very close to serious belief—why people should be encouraged to think—how helpful the Wesleyan tradition can be to people who are struggling with their faith

To this day, I remain haunted by an incident in Prague, Czechoslovakia, during the summer of 1969. I had journeyed to Prague with a group of Americans from a peace organization. Our purpose was to find out for ourselves how it was with the Czechs after the collapse of the "Prague Spring" democratic reform of 1968. Under the leadership of Alexander Dubcek, the Czechs had ventured to create a "socialism with a human face," which was an effort to combine economic socialism with political democracy. The experiment had been short-lived, however, crushed by the Soviet Union in August of that year. We arrived a few months later.

One night, two or three of us happened upon a young Czech. A philosophy student at the medieval Charles University, he told us he had been a Marxist. He was, however, deeply disillusioned—as were most of the other Czechs we had met. We had a searching conversation in which he spoke of his previous hopes. We shared our own dismay about the Vietnam War, which was then consuming American attention and resources. He was familiar with other American problems, including racism and poverty. Before parting, he asked plaintively, "What is there to believe?"

Any answer we might have framed on the spot could not have touched the depth of his disillusioned sorrow. His idealism was shattered, his faith in the world was broken. I suppose the conversation lingers so long in my memory because it captures so exactly the questioning of people the world over: "What is there to believe?"

I wrote a book during the 1980s that was framed out of such a question,[1] and my later experience with the Foundry congregation forced me to struggle even further with its implications. Here was a congregation of intelligent, well-educated people. Only partly in flattery, I remarked to them one Sunday that half the congregation could fit right into a seminary classroom with no difficulty—and the other half could be doing the teaching. But questions of belief in a seminary setting are not as exclusively academic as my comment might suggest. The Foundry congregation is made up of people confronting the deep issues of human existence; statements of belief have to be relevant to their lives, not only intellectually satisfying. In that respect, Foundry people are not all that different from honest church people everywhere. In my experience, deep theological issues can be addressed anywhere as long as theologians and pastors don't overwhelm people with unfamiliar words.

Can Ordinary Christians Use Their Minds?

It is a mystery to me why so many Christians feel apologetic about using their minds. It is almost as though many are convinced that they should leave their brains outside the door when they enter a service of worship. Even at Foundry I ran into people who seemed ashamed of their difficulty in accepting various traditional beliefs, as if they were under some obligation to believe things their minds could not accept.

Such people brought to mind yet another experience, also some years before I began my work at Foundry. I was on a panel at a southern university with the late Michael Manley, former prime minister of Jamaica. I didn't share all of his socialist convictions, but I was impressed by the quality of his mind and his obvious commitment to social justice as he understood it. He didn't wear his faith on his sleeve, but I had no doubt that he had been influenced by a church of some sort. During one of the breaks in the program, somebody asked him whether it was true that he had abandoned the Anglican Church with which he had been identified. Yes, he acknowledged sorrowfully. He had had to give up on the church because he could no longer believe in the literal virgin birth of Jesus. How extraordinary, I thought, that anybody should have to think of that as an essential belief and as the price of admission into the Christian church.

1. J. Philip Wogaman, *Faith and Fragmentation* (Philadelphia: Fortress Press, 1985).

What a loss! And how many other honest, thinking people have gone through the same sorrowful departure from a church to which they were, in other respects, strongly attracted? I resolved that if I ever served a church as pastor, nobody would have to leave over such issues of faith.

We are, of course, admonished by Scripture to love God with our minds—our God-given minds! That at least means we are not to suppress our intellectual doubts and uncertainties; we are to think our way through them. Of course, there is a kind of intellectual dilettantism that revels in doubt for its own sake. That does no service to the truth. Those who have doubts and uncertainties about serious spiritual matters recognize that they *must* struggle with them until they are resolved. Many such people have emerged with far greater spiritual insight as a fruit of their struggle. To put this all in a different way, honest doubt is seriously committed to truth, and if we believe that truth is of God then honest doubt is a form of encounter with God. Like Jacob, we often wrestle with the angel through the night, only to be blessed in the morning.

I do not think Methodists should take undue pride of possession with the so-called Wesleyan Quadrilateral, but it can be enormously helpful to people who are seeking to sort out their beliefs. I regularly emphasized the Quadrilateral in our monthly membership classes and found it opening doors of insight to many people. The Quadrilateral, briefly, is not itself a statement of belief; it is a characterization of the principal *sources* of Christian belief. As the name implies, it identifies four: Scripture, tradition, experience, and reason. The United Methodist *Book of Discipline* properly emphasizes Scripture as "primary." That is because the Bible is the most direct witness to the origins and foundation of the faith.

Nevertheless, each of the other sources is, in its own way, also primary because each interprets and criticizes the others. Scripture by itself is not sufficient (except to unthinking fundamentalists) because the Bible does not tell us how to interpret the Bible. If everything in the Bible has equal weight, that would be to equate some pretty brutal sayings with the sublime, self-giving love of Christ. Christians through history have found the gathering weight of tradition to be helpful: the formulations of ecumenical councils, the vast body of Christian hymnody, the inspiring stories of saints and martyrs, the thoughtful work of theologians. The insights of Christians of the past can be helpful in interpreting the Bible and in addressing contemporary problems of faith. But sole reliance on tradition is also unsustainable. It includes a whole lot of dangerous nonsense along with high points of insight. We have learned that some of the nonsense, like the endorsement of slavery and the preaching of crusades and inquisitions, had to be abandoned. Moreover, if tradition is to be followed uncritically, we are apt to forget one of its most distinctive marks: namely, that Christians of the past were often prepared to think new thoughts and thus to innovate.

Both Scripture and tradition are not likely to be very helpful apart from the actual experience of successive generations of Christians, so experience, both that of individual Christians and of communities of Christians, has also to be factored in as a source of theological insight. And all of this requires us to think, to use our power of reason. Some critics of the Quadrilateral wrongly consider it to be an expression of subjective individualism in theology. But experience and reason are always reflecting upon biblical and traditional sources, interpreting them in the light of the realities of ongoing history.

The Quadrilateral thus spares us the illusion that any theological formulation could be final. Or, to put this differently, it saves us from the pretension that God, having spoken once, can have nothing new to say to us. In fact, it seems to me that most theologians, no matter how conservative, really do make use of all four of those sources. It may sometimes seem untidy, with each of those four sources continuing to "speak" to the other three. But I believe that is how the church's teachings continue to instruct us.

Faith Questions

In my fifth year at Foundry, I hit upon a way of speaking quite directly to the questions people have about matters of belief. Actually, I borrowed the idea shamelessly from a clergy friend and colleague, the Rev. Donald Fado, then senior minister of St. Mark's United Methodist Church of Sacramento, California: I invited the congregation to submit written questions, which I would attempt to answer during the sermon period on a designated Sunday. I did this on one Sunday during each of my last six summers at Foundry. It went like this: The week prior to the designated Sunday, we inserted a card in each bulletin on which people were invited to write their questions (anonymously), then to drop the cards in the collection plate. A small committee of two or three lay members of the congregation was appointed to go over the submitted questions, placing them in some kind of order or priority, noting duplications and so forth. Then during the sermon period, the laypersons read me the questions they had selected, and I attempted to answer them. I began the sermon period with a very brief homily on the importance of facing our faith questions honestly, making use of a text drawn from such biblical wisdom sources as Job, Ecclesiastes, Proverbs, or, on one or two occasions, from the writings of the apostle Paul. As for the questions themselves, I never looked at them in advance, announcing to the congregation that I was hearing them for the first time just as they were. Whatever may have been lost by way of advance preparation was, I thought, more than gained through spontaneity. (Not a principle to be followed in preparation for any other sermon, I should add!) Besides, in respect to most of the questions, I had already put in quite a few years of preparation!

Was this a pretentious display of pulpit authority? I hope not. In my response to the questions, I repeatedly acknowledged my limitations. I was prepared to "take a pass" on any question that I simply could not discuss, though that never proved necessary. One of the major values of this exercise was in displaying for the congregation the range of questions on the minds of different people. Since we never had time to get through the whole batch, all of the questions were posted in a prominent place in the fellowship hall for public consideration.

While the specific formulations of questions varied somewhat from year to year, many of them were predictable. Every year there were several questions about the problem of evil and why God permits good people to suffer. Frequently there were questions about the divinity of Christ, the doctrine of the Trinity, and other classical Christian doctrines. Here is a sampling of questions from one recent year, all from different people:

> Is it a sin to worry? Does anxiety indicate a lack of faith?
>
> So many people claim to know the will of God—often with conflicting claims. If a person believes he has come to understand something of the will of God, how can he be sure that he is not suffering from a delusion or his own fanciful thinking?
>
> Why is there so much hate and insensitivity in the world? And why does politics perpetuate such hatred?
>
> Do you believe God speaks to us directly as individuals? How might that happen?
>
> How can the United Methodist Church continue to support its discriminatory positions concerning (1) the ordination of gays and lesbians, and (2) the marriage of gays and lesbians?
>
> Do you believe in a literal heaven and hell?
>
> Is it wrong for a Christian to be interested in, or even closely follow, other religions? For example, I am keenly interested in aspects of Buddhism. Is this wrong?

How do we reconcile the mandates for forgiveness and accountability? Does forgiveness mean that society shouldn't impose consequences for misbehavior?

Memory is stored physically in the brain. Does memory accompany the soul after death?

Why does God permit such serious adversities as hunger, starvation, illness, political massacre, etc., to befall large segments of the global population?

The Bible states that the way to heaven is through Christ alone. What does this mean for people of other faiths?

Do you have to believe that Jesus is *literally* the son of God (e.g., virgin birth, etc.) to be a Christian?

Do you believe that so-called near-death experiences are evidence of heaven and the Christian concept of afterlife?

The questions go on and on; over the years, perhaps there have been nearly a thousand of them. Some were repeats, in different words. Occasionally something very unexpected turned up, sometimes a direct or implied criticism (like the question, "How can you talk about our inheritance and hope—two sermons—without mentioning Jesus Christ? He is the one from whom we receive grace and who inspires us to love! Some sermons sound like those in a Unitarian church"). I tried not to respond defensively! Most of the questions were searching, clear evidence of a felt need to make sense out of the writer's faith. A number of them expressed a desire to put aside or understand better beliefs acquired much earlier in life. In responding, I sought to be respectful. A given question might seem rather naive, and yet it represented the point from which the questioner was ready to grow. A greater difficulty for me was in keeping answers reasonably succinct. My typical failure at that point meant that there was time for fewer questions, but perhaps I dodged a few bullets that way! In any case, most of the questions deserved more discussion than we could possibly give within such a format. I at least wanted to say enough to suggest possible ways of getting at an issue—enough, that is, to help people see that questions can be dealt with thoughtfully and successfully. Successfully? Some questions are deep enough that no *final* answers can be given, but that does not mean that nothing can be said on the subject, nor that we are left with sheer ignorance.

Even the short sampling of questions above reveals that people can be at very different points in their journeys of faith. Did that mean that members of the congregation would only "tune in" when their particular questions were raised? I don't think so. The process of hearing other questions voiced by other congregants was itself educational and interesting. Sometimes the questions of another person could help someone get in touch with issues he or she had long suppressed; sometimes the questions of others helped stretch the mind.

Preaching on Issues of Belief

Those faith questions were stimulating, although I was careful not to use such a format more than once a year lest the freshness and spontaneity be lost and people be tempted to think of the worship service as a college or seminary classroom. Still, some of the questions worked their way into other sermons. In order to address issues of belief in a more complete way, I found it useful to schedule a series of four or five sermons once a year. Maybe the deeper Christian beliefs point beyond themselves to mysteries that can never be fully understood intellectually. I think they do. But it is one thing to hold beliefs that transcend comprehension; it is quite another to appeal to "mystery" as a substitute for understanding. Often it is the full use of our minds that opens us up to wonderment and mystery. At any rate, in developing series of sermons on issues of belief, I hoped to contribute to greater understanding in such a way that intellectual barriers to spiritual life could be transcended. I had no illusions about being able to have the last word on these issues.

Take revelation, for instance. Is it supposed to be an arbitrary truth that one accepts on the basis of some external authority? Is it belief *imposed* upon the mind? I don't think so. Isn't it, rather, an insight that brings everything else into focus? Surely reality is more vast than anything that anybody could possibly comprehend. It is in fact quite irrational to claim to know everything! In a curious way, the wider our circle of knowledge, the greater is our confrontation with the unknown. So our perception of the overall meaning of reality has to be based upon some aspect of experience that we take to be the decisive clue. That is one way to look at revelation: It is the event or the new piece of knowledge that "unveils" reality. In a sermon on revelation, I would try to illustrate that. For example, when we enter a room of strangers we cannot know what is on their minds, whether they are hostile or friendly, what we may have in common with them. But something will be said, or we may see something in their faces, that reveals who they are and what their attitude is. We can be wrong, of course, because we can never know entirely and for sure all that lurks in the hearts of those strangers. Yet we can pick up various clues as revelations.

So it is that Christians come to the figure of Christ. People are often puzzled about a term like the *divinity* of Christ. We think we're supposed to believe in it, but what does it really mean? Are we to believe that Jesus was actually God, walking along the dusty byways of ancient Israel? If so, to whom was he praying? In particular, what did it mean for him to submit his will to God's will on that awful night when the way to the cross stretched ominously before him?

I suspect my understanding of the divinity of Christ would be quite unacceptable to some Christians, who might consider it disrespectful if not blasphemous. Yet to me, Christ is indeed divine, and I have no problem with that word. Divinity is (I think) to be understood as God at work in and through Christ. I am much attracted to the words of the apostle Paul, who speaks of how everything has changed now that God has offered us reconciliation through Christ: "All this is from God, who reconciled us to himself through Christ, and has given us the ministry of reconciliation; that is, in Christ God was reconciling the world to himself, not counting their trespasses against them, and entrusting the message of reconciliation to us" (2 Cor. 5:18–19). The human Jesus, uniquely open to God, could become the deepest revelation of the loving nature and purposes of God. People could "see" God in a new way; therefore, they could also see themselves in a new light. Does this mean that Jesus was fully human as well as divine? That has been the orthodox belief of "mainstream" churches from the beginning. It is underscored by scriptural references to Jesus' own agonizing, grieving, suffering. Indeed, is it not especially compelling that Jesus was actually *tempted?* (see Matt. 4:1–11). I take *tempted* to mean experiencing a preliminary attraction to something. I believe that Jesus' turning the temptations aside was real, not simply a well-acted scene in a preformatted drama. God, thus revealed through the faithfulness and goodness of a real human being, is much more compelling to me!

Perhaps there lurks here a way to deal with the ever more urgent issue of how Christians are to relate to other faiths. One of the faith questions that recurred year after year was how to understand that passage from the Fourth Gospel: "I am the way, and the truth, and the life. No one comes to the Father except through me" (John 14:6). Those who are not biblical literalists can, of course, simply note that the Gospel of John is a theological interpretation of the meaning of Christ and not a tape recording of Jesus' actual words. Yet there may be a deeper truth in the words themselves. If one truly believes that the reality of God is expressed through Christ, then that reality is surely "the way, and the truth, and the life." God, named here as "Father," is pure, unqualified love. It is the self-giving love of Christ that provides us the decisive clue to the character of God. Is that also a possibility in other cultural settings, for people with different cultural histories? I am not enough of an authority on other cultural settings to give a rounded answer to that, except to say that I know of no culture on earth where human love is totally absent. Is it not presumptuous to deny the work of God in settings other than those shaped by Christian faith? And, as a Christian, should I not always identify genuine love as the work of God?

The Dialogue with Muslims

These issues about Christ took on new urgency for Foundry people in the aftermath of September 11, 2001. One of our first instincts at Foundry was to reach out to the growing Muslim community in America with understanding and caring. We wanted them to know that we were not holding Islam as a whole responsible for those awful deeds done by a handful of Muslims. Two Foundry members, Jim Leader and Jim Viterello, were especially sensitive to the feelings of our Muslim fellow citizens, and so they helped facilitate a dialogue with people from the Dar al-Hijrah Mosque in nearby Falls Church, Virginia. The format was simple. The Muslims invited Foundry people to come to their mosque on a Sunday afternoon in late 2001 for a repast and discussion time. A Muslim scholar gave an informative overview of Islam and answered questions from Foundry members. I said a few things about Christianity, emphasizing the gospel of love and reading Paul's great words on love in 1 Corinthians 13 in their entirety. About sixty of the Muslims and sixty of the Methodists then gathered in small groups around tables, exchanging thoughts and questions. Then in January 2002, we invited Muslims to Foundry, with a similar format except that I made the principal presentation.

Such encounters may only scratch the surface of mutual understanding. Yet a decisive issue presented itself. The Muslim leaders spoke of the prophet Muhammad with great reverence, while insisting that their faith was not about him but about the Holy Qur'an, which had been dictated to him by Allah, word for word. The Qur'an contains the correct teaching about human life; we are to submit to it wholeheartedly, they said. The Muslim scholars were very clear about their esteem for other faiths, including Christianity. They regard Moses, the Hebrew prophets, and Jesus as prophets whose teachings are worthy of respect. The issue they had with Christianity was that we are centered on a person (Christ) and that our doctrine of the Trinity is a denial of the fundamental unity of God.

We helped clarify this last point, for Christianity is also monotheistic. Whatever else one may say about the doctrine of the Trinity, it is not about three gods. (A better shorthand statement of the Trinity is that it is about one God expressed in three ways. More needs to be said, of course, but that point of clarification is necessary.) But, at least to me, the deeper issue was one they had also raised most clearly: Islam is about *teachings* of God, transmitted through the prophet Muhammad, while Christianity is about the *person* of Christ as an authentic revelation of the nature of God.

I'm not sure all Muslims would agree with those with whom we were in dialogue, but insofar as they would, this is indeed a watershed issue. Christians do consider Christ to be central. It is not that Christ is "a god," but neither is it that Christ was simply a compelling teacher of moral and spiritual wisdom. It is in Christ that we see what love really is and that it is from God. That is different from teaching *about* love, although the teaching surely has its place. We didn't get into the distinction between grace and works of the law, so central to the apostle Paul, but that distinction is surely at work when religious faith is portrayed primarily as teachings and rules to be followed rather than primarily as love to which we are invited to respond. We love because he first loved us—we don't do works of love just because we think we ought to.

Much more could be said. These dialogue occasions, valuable as they were, were only preliminary. I am confident that in the process of obeying the teachings of the Qur'an to do works of kindness and mercy, many Muslims are drawn into actual love that transcends external teachings and works. I am equally sure that many Christians, supposedly devoted to the figure of Christ, lack the self-discipline needed to make the love of Christ more than sentimental feeling.

Myth and Metaphor

Behind all of the specific issues of faith there lies the deeper question: How can we *know* the truth? If by *truth* we mean ideas that convey reality, the simple but lamentable answer is that we cannot say that we *know*. As the apostle Paul puts it, "Now we see in a mirror, dimly" and "Now I know only in part" (1 Cor. 13:12). And as the Epistle to the Hebrews reminds us, "Faith is the assurance of things hoped for, the conviction of things not seen" (Heb. 11:1). It is faith, not final knowledge of ultimate reality, that gives us the assurance to carry on. Still, it is not blind faith. It is faith drawn forth from some kinds of evidence, nurtured by traditions, sustained by communities of faith.

In working with a community of faith like Foundry Church, I, like all pastors, had to confront a dilemma. On the one hand, I had to be perfectly honest about the limitations of our knowledge; I had to be clear that some kinds of belief, though perpetuated through centuries of tradition, are not sustainable in literal form. On the other hand, belief in the truthfulness of inherited and shared traditions is vital to our faith, and thus to be preached with confidence.

Theologians have long understood that ultimate truths can be conveyed in the form of myth. To the average person, a myth may simply seem to be untrue because it is about something that never happened. But religious myths, while sometimes framed as specific events that never happened, may still express a truth that is deeper than fact. Jesus himself often taught by means of stories (parables) that were not about actual events but that expressed truth. The stories of the Good Samaritan and the Prodigal Son, through constant retelling, have all the flavor of real occurrence. Yet we know they were but stories to convey larger truths—the first about our common humanity, despite differences of nationality and ethnicity, the second about the loving and forgiving character of God. The Hebrew books of Jonah and Ruth, though portrayed as factual, are believed by most knowledgeable scholars to have been stories designed in large measure to counteract ethnocentric tendencies during the period in which they were written.

Once or twice I preached directly about the meaning of myth. On other occasions I briefly sought to indicate the difference between the literal details of story and tradition and the deeper truths being conveyed. I'm not sure my efforts were always successful. With many people, the connection between literal detail and deeper meaning is just too tight. The broad picture can scarcely be perceived by some unless they also have confidence in the details. My greatest concern was usually with the broad picture, with the deeper truths, and therefore I tried not to be too confrontational in challenging the literalisms some found necessary. Yet my lingering impression is that a majority of the people were greatly helped by honesty in these matters. People who have already abandoned the faith because they can no longer believe the literal details of a particular tradition cannot regain their faith by becoming literalists again! They are ready to move on, into deeper currents of believing. I think there are many such people today, and I know that more than a few of the people attracted to Foundry were like that.

An important part of being honest about tradition is a recognition that all belief about ultimate reality is metaphorical in character.[2] That is to say, since the nature of the whole of reality is beyond full comprehension (we "know only in part"), what we *believe* about the whole of reality will be based upon the things we find compelling. That, as I have already noted, is what revelation finally comes down to. The words in Christian devotion used to describe God, for instance, are derived from experience. God can be characterized as the *rock* of our salvation—not meaning that God is literally a rock, but that, like a rock, God endures, is not easily moved, is dependable. When God is referred to as *Father*, it is not that God is literally a biological being. But the intimate relationship of a good father to his children is something like God's relationship with human beings. As I noted in a Mother's Day sermon in 1993, God can as well be characterized as mother, but again not in the literal biological sense. Theologian Paul Tillich remarked that the only nonsymbolic statement about God is to characterize God as "being-itself." All that gives *content* to our understanding of God is symbolic or metaphorical.[3]

The challenge to preaching is how to use stories and metaphors to express deeper truths without being sidetracked by questions of literal fact. I found that in preaching one needs to be as clear as possible about this in order to get sophisticated people beyond the purely factual level. A forest is comprised of trees, and yet attention to individual trees alone can distract us from experiencing the depth of the forest. I myself am most moved by a great preacher's free use of metaphor, and yet the power of a metaphor can be diminished if the preacher conveys that he or she takes it to be literally descriptive. A great preacher is steeped in biblical imagery, but that imagery also loses power when accompanied by assumptions of biblical literalism.

2. I have explored the implications of this more fully in *Faith and Fragmentation*.

3. "The statement that God is being-itself is a nonsymbolic statement. . . . It means what it says directly and properly; if we speak of the actuality of God, we first assert that he is not God if he is not being-itself. . . . There can be no doubt that any concrete assertion about God must be symbolic, for a concrete assertion is one which uses a segment of finite experience in order to say something about him." Paul Tillich, *Systematic Theology*, vol. 1 (Chicago: University of Chicago Press, 1951), 238–39. This quotation itself employs metaphor in Tillich's use of *he* and *him* as pronouns referring to God.

Chapter Eight

Becoming a Reconciling Congregation

In which I am drawn into a sharp internal debate at Foundry on an explosive issue—reflect on the "baggage" I brought to the question—recall the church's long study process, anxieties about the impending vote, and how a congregation struggled with conflict—acknowledge God's "mixed blessing"

I knew before going to Foundry that the church was facing an important decision about whether or not to become a "Reconciling Congregation." The designation is entirely unofficial in the United Methodist Church. It was adopted by an unofficial coalition of churches to express their openness to gay and lesbian people. Implicitly, Reconciling Congregations are understood to be critical of the denomination's official position on homosexuality, although a church designating itself in that way might simply be signaling a welcome to gay and lesbian people. Such a welcoming stance is entirely consistent with the denomination's official position that all people need the ministries of the church. But there was a problem with part of the rest of the official teaching, which was adopted at the 1972 General Conference and modified only slightly since then. In 1992, as I entered Foundry, the denominational position read as follows:

> Homosexual persons no less than heterosexual persons are individuals of sacred worth. All persons need the ministry and guidance of the Church in their struggles for human fulfillment, as well as the spiritual and emotional care of a fellowship which enables reconciling relationships with God, with others, and with self. *Although we do not condone the practice of homosexuality and consider this practice*

> *incompatible with Christian teaching*, we affirm that God's grace is available to all. We commit ourselves to be in ministry for and with all persons.[1] (italics added)

A Reconciling Congregation could be understood to fulfill all of this quite directly, except for the words asserting that the "practice of homosexuality" is "incompatible with Christian teaching." The full implications of this judgmental language became evident in 1984 when the General Conference adopted a provision that no "self-avowed, practicing homosexual" could be ordained or appointed to a pastorate. This was not only a teaching; it was church law. Reconciling Congregations were understood to be at odds with such teaching and law; theirs was a position of implied dissent.

Foundry's struggle with the issue of homosexuality had begun several years before my arrival in 1992. By the mid-1970s, several gay and lesbian people had begun to identify with the church. In 1977, my predecessor, Dr. Bauman, preached a widely noted sermon, "Reflections on the Gay Life," in which he called for greater sensitivity to the humanity and feelings of gay and lesbian people:

> We love them as persons. We stand beside them and share the burden of pain which society has laid upon them. For those who are troubled with their condition and want to be "healed," we help them find that healing through the power of God in Jesus Christ and in whatever ways he makes available to us. To those who do not want to be "healed" and are insulted by the suggestion, we offer God's love and our love. We listen to them and learn from them.

The sermon was greatly appreciated in the gay and lesbian community and was, on the whole, well received by the congregation. Increasingly the church became known as hospitable to gay and lesbian people.

In 1990 a member of the church's Council on Missions proposed that the church should identify with the Reconciling Congregation movement. A representative task force of church members was established to study the implications such a decision would have for the church. Dr. Flemming, highly respected by everybody, became its chair. At the beginning of this process, well before there was any thought of my becoming senior minister at Foundry, I was asked to address a Sunday morning forum. My assignment was to brief Foundry people on how the denomi-

1. *The Book of Discipline of The United Methodist Church*, 1992, para. 71, G.

nation as a whole was studying the issue of homosexuality. Subsequent forums revealed sharp disagreements within the church. Representatives of the "Transforming Congregation" movement, supported by a few Foundry families, urged the church to reject the Reconciling Congregation proposal and substitute an agenda seeking to change homosexuals. In early 1991, Dr. Bauman sent a pastoral letter to all Foundry members in which he affirmed his personal conviction that gay and lesbian people should be accepted without discrimination. Nevertheless, in light of the divisions he perceived in the church, he urged Foundry not to become a Reconciling Congregation.

The task force proceeded for the two years prior to my coming to Foundry. Initially it had been thought that this study process could be completed in a year or so. In fact, it was nowhere near finishing its work when I arrived. Since the senior minister was an ex officio member of the task force, I replaced Dr. Bauman for what turned out to be three more years of the group's study.

My History on the Issue

On this issue, I didn't have to start from scratch! As a matter of fact, it was fairly well known that I brought a certain amount of baggage with me on issues related to homosexuality. When it took notice of my appointment to Foundry, the *Washington Post* emphasized the leadership I had been giving on those issues at the denominational level. It was well known that my stance was basically liberal. In my first year or so at Foundry, I said comparatively little about homosexuality from the pulpit, however. People knew I could speak to that; the only question in some minds was whether I could preach about anything else!

I am not sure very many people knew much about my own journey in dealing with homosexuality. I certainly did not start out with a very liberal viewpoint. At the beginning of my teaching career, around 1960, my view was that homosexuality was either some form of sin or some form of sickness or some mixture of both. I couldn't be sure which was the dominant factor, but it was one or the other or both of these human failings. These views were reinforced by the institutional policies of Wesley Theological Seminary in my early years there. Psychological tests were administered to all incoming students, with an eye toward identifying and dealing with pathologies, prominent among which was homosexuality. I knew of a handful of cases in which incoming students with homosexual tendencies were required to undergo change therapy, and I can even recall one such case in which a student later expressed appreciation for what he considered to be successful therapy. I have no idea how others worked out. During my years as dean of the seminary, I had to deal with two or three situations administratively. One was of a prospective student who seemed altogether too preoccupied—I would almost say obsessed—by his own sexual orientation. We rejected his application on the supposition that he was too focused on sex. In another case, the story of an older student was splashed all over the *Washington Post* and the *Evening Star* after he left his family and a small northern Virginia parish he was then serving as a student pastor, announcing that there were numbers of closeted homosexuals in the church and at the seminary. Considering his behavior altogether irresponsible, we encouraged his departure from the seminary. In yet another situation, a woman student leader announced her homosexuality and entered into a committed union with another woman in a public ceremony. She was, I think, quite convinced that the seminary would never grant her degree. I believed at the time that her actions were evidence of emotional needs, not of actual homosexuality. In any event, it would have been quite irresponsible of the seminary to prevent her from graduating—so I greeted her with a warm handshake and a smile after she was handed her diploma. Years later she looked me up to say that she had left the homosexual life, convinced that it was morally wrong.

Such cases probably reinforced my earlier views about homosexuality. Even so, as a professional Christian ethicist I simply wasn't all that interested in the issue. If homosexuality was a sin, it was not a major one. If it was a sickness, it certainly wasn't all that disabling for its victims. It was, perhaps, a misfortune for those who were involved. As an ethicist, I considered the great economic and political issues of our time and racism to be much more important. In that era, when a cold war threatened global catastrophe and, in this most wealthy country on earth, thirty to forty million people still were locked in poverty, it seemed a bit self-indulgent to spend much time on homosexuality.

I kept no log of my changing attitude. It began in the late 1970s and continued in the 1980s. In part it was rooted in my efforts to be responsive to the questions of students, for whom this was an issue of gathering importance. In part it was in reaction to the obvious overemphasis of conservatives, whose preoccupations with sexual issues seemed to me to be at least as unhealthy as I had thought those of homosexuals to be. That came to a focus for me at the United Methodist General Conference of 1984 when, from the galleries, I witnessed delegates enact a sweeping rule that "self-avowed practicing homosexuals" could not be ordained or appointed as pastors. To single homosexual behavior out in this way, while ignoring a whole lot of other things, just seemed wrong to me. I also began to feel that conservative critics of homosexual behavior were expressing views that could not be sustained by available knowledge. I, at least, had to acknowledge that I simply did not know why some people are homosexual and others are not. That is, of course, a central question.

I had to face the issues more seriously when I was elected as a delegate to the 1988 General Conference and began receiving what seemed an avalanche of letters expressing views on issues related to homosexuality. Most of these were emotional but not well supported intellectually and therefore not convincing. They helped me see how important the homosexuality question had become in the life of our denomination—but also how confused it seemed to be. The situation seemed ripe for a really thorough study process. I helped formulate a resolution expressing the United Methodist Church's quandary and establishing a study committee charged with exploring the biblical, theological, and factual aspects of the question and reporting back to the 1992 General Conference. The committee was instructed to use expert consultants, and funds were to be provided for that purpose. The resolution was adopted, and the committee was formed. It began its work in late 1988 and met regularly for two or three days at a time until its final report was prepared in 1991.

When asked to serve on this committee, I readily agreed. I trusted that the process would answer some of my own questions.[2] In some respects it

2. The people who made up the committee were, for the most part, highly competent and representative of the different demographic categories of our denomination. In retrospect, I think the committee was, with a couple of dozen members, about twice too large. It was also, in my judgment, weighted too heavily toward those seeking to liberalize the church's position. At times I therefore had to help ensure that the views of conservative members were being dealt with fairly and that issues were being addressed with rigorous honesty. In the end, the committee's report was scrupulously careful in its treatment of issues. Critics who sought to dismiss the committee's work because of the liberal disposition of most of its members could not honestly ignore the report itself. There were not many conservatives on the committee, but those who were, joined with the rest of us on most of the report's findings. An ideal committee would have included two or three well-known conservatives, an equal number of liberals, and a balance of six or eight well-respected leaders who could be counted upon to render honest conclusions. Such a committee could perhaps have included a self-identified homosexual and, perhaps, a self-identified "ex-gay." Consensus arrived at in such a committee might have commanded greater support at the 1992 General Conference. However, the work of the actual committee was certainly worthy of such support. In printed form it remains an unusually clear delineation of the issues.

did; in other respects it did not. It did help clarify the relationship between questions of faith and questions of fact. Factual data cannot, in themselves, provide ethical conclusions. The issues we were struggling with could not simply be turned over to psychology or biology or sociology for solution. What *is* may not conform to what *ought to be.* What we *want* may not at all be what we truly *need.* Thus, some people may have a biological predisposition toward alcoholism, but that would not mean that this is normal, much less that it is good. Some of the conservative critics of homosexual practice have agreed that there are people who are born with a disposition toward homosexuality, and if so this is a problem they should be helped to get over. But *why* is it a problem? Most conservatives with whom we spoke either resolved that by virtue of a special biblical or theological claim or, ironically, by appealing to scientific data suggesting the abnormality of homosexuality. One of the conservative members of the committee seemed to fluctuate back and forth between a kind of biblical reasoning and a form of natural law ethic that appeals to natural reason.

Most of us came to understand that there is a clearer way to relate faith to fact. It is, in brief, to acknowledge our deepest faith convictions about what is ultimately good. For a Christian, that is bound to refer somehow to a love that is based finally upon God's grace (or unqualified love) as revealed through Jesus Christ. Then we are in a position to ask what are the factual conditions that support or obstruct the fulfillment of the life of love within ourselves and in our relationship with God and one another. We can then pursue, in a meaningful way, the question whether there is anything about the "practice of homosexuality" that supports or obstructs such fulfillment.

We met with a number of knowledgeable scientific consultants, but unfortunately none of them—nor our reading of scientific literature—brought closure to the issue of why some people are and others are not homosexual or heterosexual in orientation. There is not yet any broad consensus about that among scientists. Some are persuaded that it is a matter of natural inheritance, genetically determined. Others conclude that it is a matter of early experience. I confess I was disappointed to discover that there is no conclusive answer to why homosexuality exists. I had hoped science would help settle that for us. At two points, however, the scientists were indeed helpful: first, in the conclusive evidence that homosexuality is experienced by most homosexuals as involuntary (and often from very early age); and second, that apparently many if not most gay and lesbian people are not able to change their orientation, try as they might.

But if the scientists could not bring closure, the committee discovered a form of evidence that was closer at hand and more helpful. We had a chance to get acquainted with gay and lesbian people who clearly evidenced the power of God's love in their own lives. That helped answer the question whether there is anything about homosexuality that *necessarily* inhibits the receiving of God's love, freely given, or in expressing that love in commitments and relationships. We discovered that there are numbers of self-avowed practicing Christians who are also homosexual. That obviously could not apply to anyone whose homosexuality was the very center of his or her existence, any more than it could be true of a heterosexual whose ultimate values were sexual. But for those whose lives are oriented toward a deeper spirituality, it seems increasingly clear that homosexual expressions of love can be positive and healthy.[3]

Not everybody supports that view, of course. But in light of the clouded state of the question there might at least be a deeper level of tolerance born out of intellectual humility. In the absence of demonstrable truth, a basic rule might be, "First, do not hurt."

Such thoughts were occupying my mind when, shortly after the 1992 General Conference (which simply reaffirmed the old restrictive rules), I arrived at Foundry and became a part of Foundry's ongoing study of whether to become a Reconciling Congregation. I soon became acquainted with numbers of gay and lesbian members who absolutely underscored the conclusion that such people can be good, decent, morally disciplined, unselfish, Spirit-filled Christians the same as anybody else.

The Process Comes to a Conclusion

In my first year I didn't say much about homosexuality from the pulpit. On one or two occasions I did remark that it is an inescapable part of the description of a church that it be *reconciling*, in the broad sense of the word—

3. I was greatly moved by a statement of the great South African archbishop Desmond Tutu, which I came upon after we had finished this work: "[W]e claim that sexuality is a divine gift, which used properly, helps us to become more fully human and akin really to God, as it is this part of our humanity that makes us more gentle and caring, more self-giving and concerned for others than we would be without that gift. Why should we want all homosexual persons not to give expression to their sexuality in loving acts? Why don't we use the same criteria to judge same-sex relationships that we use to judge whether heterosexual relationships are wholesome or not?" Foreword to Marilyn Bennett Alexander and James Preston, *We Were Baptized Too* (Louisville, Ky.: Westminster John Knox Press, 1996).

just as a church is also called to be *transforming*, for that matter. The issue before the church, I said, is what we choose to call ourselves. On that, I was prepared to respect the conclusions yet to be reached by Foundry's study committee and the church's official Administrative Board. I remarked on one occasion that we could be clear about two things: first, that we don't really know yet why people are gay or lesbian or heterosexual; and second, that there are some very good people who are gay and lesbian, including some who were members of Foundry Church.

The study process continued for another three years. It was organized around the preparation of what came to be a book-length report, with chapters dealing with different aspects of the question of homosexuality, including the church's history with the subject, the scriptural and theological issues, and the implications of being a Reconciling Congregation. Along the way, open hearings were held to give progress reports and to provide an opportunity for church members to express their feelings. The hearings during the last three years of the study were, on the whole, quite civil and without undue conflict. I was told that some earlier hearings had been a good deal more acrimonious.

Even after five years it proved difficult to bring the process to closure, partly because a couple of the key chapters had to be rewritten several times to satisfy the task force. I think it was also because some church leaders felt any decision by the church would alienate a certain number of members. It might be better, some thought, just to keep the process going.

That was not my own judgment. I thought it would be better to get the decision, the long-anticipated "vote," behind us and move on. Prompted in part by similar thinking by our lay leader (who was not a member of the committee), I began to emphasize our need to bring the process to closure.[4] That meant that within the task force we would have to vote on

4. While it was obviously time for us to move beyond the stage of study and discussion, I must confess that my own sense of timing was partly influenced by the presidential election calendar. If the matter were to be decided a few months later, on the very eve of the 1996 presidential election, that could invite the wrong kind of publicity on this inflamed issue, since both prospective major party candidates had had significant relationships with our church. Neither President Clinton nor Senator Dole had been involved in any way in the Reconciling Congregation issue, either in our study process or in the congregation's impending decision. But that would not have prevented demagogic critics from using this to embarrass the president or senator. Reaching a decision over a year in advance of the elections allowed time for matters to cool down. Senator Dole had ended his relationship with Foundry by October 1995, but neither he nor President Clinton voiced any criticism of the study process or of the church's decision.

some things, allowing a majority to determine the outcome rather than waiting for an elusive unanimity. The committee responded to this and moved toward a conclusion of its study. The matter went before the church's Council on Ministries and received an initial hearing by the Administrative Board, with the understanding that the final vote would be taken at the October 1995 meeting.

While not wishing to influence the outcome of all this unduly, I did weigh in at two points. First, when a draft resolution was presented to the Council on Ministries, I encouraged the council to include a recognition that the church remained fully accepting of members who disagreed with our becoming a Reconciling Congregation. I made the point that we could hardly be in a position of rejecting members who agreed with the denomination's view on homosexuality, even though it was becoming evident that most members of the church wanted to be more accepting of gay and lesbian people. Second, I encouraged informal negotiation between people with different viewpoints to see whether mutually acceptable compromises could be worked out. These discussions were not between those who supported the Reconciling Congregation approach as opposed to the Transforming Congregation option[5]—very few Foundry members wanted anything to do with that second option. Rather, it was between those who wished to identify the church fully with the organized Reconciling Congregation movement and those who wished to affirm the same stance but without the specific label and institutional commitments. It didn't prove possible to work out a compromise on this issue, so it came down to a decision between two approaches to the same basic objective: a church publicly committed to full acceptance of gay and lesbian people.

As the Administrative Board members assembled for the decisive meeting on October 3, I was reminded of the way an airline pilot described his job: 98 percent boredom and 2 percent terror. There is nothing particularly terrifying about church board meetings, but the boredom factor is another matter. Still, when a hot issue is on the table, people can get excited. So it was no surprise that we had a very large turnout that night, with around a hundred members on hand. The leadership had structured a supper and opportunity for table conversation for groups of eight or ten. Then we all assembled for debate. Four proposals were placed before the body in resolution form: One declared Foundry to be a Reconciling Congregation,

5. The "Transforming Congregation" movement sought to recruit congregations committed to "transforming" homosexual persons into heterosexual persons. Such churches were not to accept homosexuality as a "given" at any point.

with the implication of full participation in the national network. A second supported full inclusion of gay and lesbian people, committed the church to working to change denominational policy toward that end, but stopped short of using the Reconciling Congregation label or participating in the national network. A third, diametrically opposed to these two, was in the spirit of the Transforming Congregation model. A fourth somewhat ambiguously sought healing on the issue but without specifics.

In the debate, three or four people expressed support for the Transforming Congregation model with its "homosexuality is immoral" theme. The person who had proposed that alternative, having had her say, withdrew that proposal. Most members were in favor of one of the first two options. The debate was conducted in a civil way, with the chairperson, Adele Hutchins, wisely allowing it to proceed for a couple of hours without the constraints of parliamentary legalism. When the debate wound down and it was time to make a decision, the board, on recommendation of the lay leader, took a novel approach. Each of the remaining three options would be voted up or down in turn, beginning with the Reconciling Congregation proposal since it had come to the board with the formal backing of the church's Council on Ministries. If it had failed, the second option would then have been put to a vote. The vote was taken by secret ballot. While tellers counted the votes, board members waited in quiet conversation. I was to be informed of the results first so I could, as pastor, interpret the outcome. As it turned out, there was no need for a second vote. The Reconciling Congregation proposal had a majority of the votes: 56 to 49.

That was a close vote, and I briefly pondered whether I should encourage further postponement for the sake of a clearer consensus. Or it might have been possible to turn to the second option since that could have been adopted almost unanimously if it had been the only proposal considered. On reflection, however, it seemed to me that an attempt to set aside the majority's decision would have led to greater long-run tensions in the church. I did feel, however, that all of the next moves needed to be in the direction of reassuring those who had serious doubts or anxieties about our becoming a Reconciling Congregation that the church had room for dissenters on this issue, and that, in fact, we needed to continue the dialogue. I announced the results to the board and spent some time with interpretation along those lines.

The following Sunday we announced the results to the congregation at both worship services, again encouraging members to feel they did not have to agree in order to be fully accepted in the congregation. To be a

Reconciling Congregation certainly had to mean that there was room for people who agreed with the present denominational stance as well as for those who agreed with the majority vote in the Administrative Board. The language of the resolution adopted by the board sought to convey something of that spirit:

STATEMENT OF RECONCILIATION

> We, the friends and members of Foundry United Methodist Church, hold deeply our commitment to help bring about a peaceful, loving, just and accepting world. We are proud of our active, diverse congregation and have seen how each person has graced our community with his or her talents. We believe that the Holy Spirit dwells in all.
>
> We acknowledge our oneness with all of God's creation and invite gay and lesbian persons to share our faith, our community life and our ministries. We also affirm the same for all persons without regard to race, color, national origin, gender, sexual orientation, marital status, age, economic status, or physical or mental condition. We seek to be an inclusive congregation, and we proclaim our commitment to seek the reconciliation of all persons to God and to each other through Jesus Christ.
>
> As we journey toward reconciliation with all, we proclaim this statement of welcome to all, including our gay and lesbian brothers and sisters: God loves you and we love you, we affirm you, we accept you, we treasure you. We welcome you.
>
> At the same time, we recognize that there remain differences of opinion among us on issues relating to sexuality. We do not seek to erase our differences, but to journey together in faith toward greater understanding and mutual respect.
>
> In becoming a Reconciling Congregation we believe that we are being reconciled to God and to one another. "All this is from God, who reconciled us . . . through Christ, and has given us the ministry of reconciliation." (II Corinthians 5:18)

The Lasting Effects

Most of the opposition to Foundry's declaring itself a Reconciling Congregation was, in my judgment, prompted more by institutional concerns than substantive objection to our being nonjudgmentally receptive to gay and lesbian people. I will have to admit that I shared some of the institutional anxieties, even while fully supporting the decision. Would the church lose members? Would it be labeled and dismissed as a "gay church," and thereby suffer from the well-known prejudices of many people on this subject? Later I came to believe that an important part of carrying the cross of Christ is willingness to share the stigma attached to people who are often rejected. Our experience helped me to see that the willingness to share the stigma of rejected people was no small part of why Christ himself was rejected by the religious elites of his day.

But I should not have worried at all. True, over a period of months several people chose to withdraw, in spite of our efforts to encourage them to stay. But many more people were attracted to the church. That predictably included increased numbers of gay and lesbian people, but it also included numbers of others who were attracted to Foundry as a progressive, inclusive congregation. Whatever fears any had over scandalous behavior by gay or lesbian members proved to be utterly groundless. To my knowledge—and I think I was in a position to know—there just weren't *any* incidents of that sort. The gay and lesbian people who were attracted to Foundry wanted a normal church environment in which they would be fully accepted but not be the center of attention. They appeared to me to be quite as psychologically normal and morally self-disciplined as anybody else. Some have emerged as creative, energetic leaders of great talent and good judgment. Occasionally a gay or lesbian person would remark that this was the first time in many years he or she had felt accepted by a church. I grieve over the implications of that concerning their previous experiences, even as I feel very good about what Foundry has been able to be and do. Meanwhile, in a downtown environment in which membership in many churches was declining precipitously, Foundry continued to be a vibrant presence, attracting many people and engaging in its mission faithfully. I doubt that would have been possible if we had turned our back upon gay and lesbian people and persons of other minority groups. But the deeper reasons for what we did are set forth in the church's "Statement of Reconciliation."

A final, somewhat surprising result can be recorded: When it became clear that Foundry was fully accepting and that I, as senior minister, was in full support of that as fundamental to our identity as a church, it then became possible to be fully pastoral with those struggling with questions of sexual orientation. In a fully accepting environment it was possible for gay and lesbian people to work through their issues. I don't know why I should have been surprised by that, but it reinforced the insight that it is when we are surrounded by rigidity that we are less free to confront problems within ourselves that we ought to be facing.

I conclude from this that even if it were to be found beyond question that homosexuality is not a natural or desirable state of being, it would be considerably easier for homosexuals to change if they were not confronting a repressive environment. Thus, even if the conservatives in the church should prove to be right in their negative assessment of homosexuality, I would still conclude they are fundamentally wrong in the legalistic atmosphere they have sought to create to deal with it. Having said this, I believe the weight of evidence—including that derived from a considerable amount of pastoral experience—is that the conservatives are also wrong in their negative assessment. But whether or not that is so, I plead with them to ease up on the moralism and repressive church legislation. It isn't very Christian!

Chapter Nine

Meeting the Press

In which I gain experience in dealing with the media, much of it the hard way—respond to attacks from the right—encounter unique opportunities and spiritual dangers—form some judgments about the current state of American print and broadcast journalism

Even before going to Foundry I occasionally had dealt with the press. As a seminary professor and dean I had taken positions on controversial issues attracting some attention, and I was sometimes called upon to help interpret current events from an ethical perspective. I had also played a role on two high-profile issues in our denomination—the Nestlé boycott and the homosexuality study—that entailed interaction with the press. But I was to discover a whole new dimension to press relations after arriving at Foundry. As a new pastor, I found this to be both energizing and intimidating.

My first major encounter with the press after beginning my pastorate began in 1992 with the crisis concerning my predecessor. As I mentioned earlier, church leadership learned the importance of not trying to hide information from the press, even while we appealed to the journalists' sense of responsibility. In subsequent years, media attention and inquiries came with increasing frequency, in part because of the Clintons' growing relationship with Foundry. Other press inquiries through the early years included an occasional newspaper, radio, or television interview related to a general religious topic, such as the observance of Christmas or Easter at our church. These conversations were probably as boring to the interviewers as they doubtless were to many readers or listeners, and I'm not sure what I could have done to make them more interesting. Of course, journalists try to make things interesting by concentrating on conflict and controversy, and that is certainly one method. A better approach might have been to work at establishing the relevance of religious themes to the problems and decisions people face in ordinary life and to the values and goals implicit in the public sphere.

I have to confess that I felt flattered by attention from *Newsweek* magazine after the Clintons began attending Foundry. The veteran *Newsweek* writer Kenneth Woodward spent two or three hours with me clarifying the role of Methodist tradition on Hillary Clinton's religious attitudes, part of which I could confirm and part of which I had to correct based on my own reading of the tradition. Woodward had an engaging mind and struck me as a moderately conservative Roman Catholic but with a distinctly ecumenical attitude. The article was responsibly done.

More controversial media encounters grew out of criticisms of our church and of me in particular from the religious right wing. Our most persistent critic was the Institute for Religion and Democracy. The IRD had its origins in the Cold War climate of the 1970s, when its stock-in-trade was criticism of the ecumenical movement and religious bodies and leaders who appeared to be too soft on communism. When the Cold War ended, the IRD had to find other targets, which came to include those who were on the liberal side of abortion and homosexuality issues. Its political agenda became clear in its efforts to get at President Clinton by attacking the church he was attending. One early piece, by the IRD's Mark Tooley, focused on the background of the person President Clinton was hearing from the pulpit. I was sent a copy of the article for corrective comment by its author, which I ignored. It came at an unusually busy time; I really didn't have time to attend to the many errors and distortions in the article. Besides, I just didn't trust the writer. I feared that if I responded in any way it would only add fuel to the fire. My intuition about that was confirmed by two or three church leaders who believed they had themselves been treated irresponsibly by this writer. Still, in retrospect, I regret that I didn't take the time, no matter how busy I was, to go through the article patiently and offer corrections. If I had done so, I would have noted four kinds of statements: those which truthfully reflected my past actions and views I continue to affirm, those items which, while accurate, represented things about which I had changed my mind; those which were just inaccurate; and those which, while factually accurate, were taken out of context and therefore untrue.

I have to thank Mr. Tooley for helping to sharpen my perspective on the ethics of journalism, even though mostly by illustrating its abuses. He had gone over a number of my books, written over a period of more than twenty-five years, looking for a sentence here, a paragraph there, that could be used as negative evidence of what the president must be hearing from the pulpit. The result was utterly irresponsible journalism, but it had one effect that became quite memorable. It was picked up by the widely syndicated columnist, Cal Thomas, who reduced it to column-size length and put it out as his own work in hundreds of newspapers across the land. I was appalled. While the IRD wasn't all that prominent, Cal Thomas had millions of readers. Through intermediaries we attempted to get a correction of the most egregious errors. The response from the columnist was that I could write letters to the editor. To five hundred newspapers? I did send a reply, which was probably too lengthy, to fifteen or twenty leading papers. To my knowledge, only one used it. Standing back from that episode with the further experience of several more years, I think I shouldn't have worried about the effect of even that kind of unfriendly exposure. The moment went away quickly; there was no lasting harm. In fact, it may have been a good counterbalance to equally overstated praise I was getting from other quarters! I was reminded once again of Bishop Yeakel's advice in a different context: "Don't inhale!"

There is a postscript to the Cal Thomas episode. A few years later, I was asked to be on CNN's *Crossfire.* I had been on *Crossfire* a couple of other times. Its format at the time exemplified some of the worst aspects of TV talk shows. Essentially, two people who hold views radically different from two other people faced off, with much interruption and no opportunity for thoughtful reflection on the issues. I had been encouraged by Carolyn never to be a part of that kind of thing again, but this particular *Crossfire* program was to have a different format. It would be recorded several days before Christmas and would air on Christmas day, with a quieter reflection on the state of American Christianity at this Christmas time. It sounded all right, so I accepted. Opposite me was to be Ralph Reed, then the young leader of the Christian Coalition. I then learned that he had backed out, not wanting to appear with a liberal pastor. Cal Thomas had been invited as a substitute. I recounted my history with Cal Thomas but agreed to participate. When I appeared at the studio, he greeted me warmly and presented me with a nicely wrapped Christmas gift book. After the program, which went reasonably well as *Crossfire* goes, I invited Thomas to lunch. He accepted, and we had an affable conversation during which neither of us mentioned the column. Maybe it was good for both of us to experience each other as real people.

The IRD revealed its basic character on yet another occasion. Foundry had agreed to be a host for the biannual Rainbow of Light Conference.

That event, including speakers, worship, and workshops, focuses on ministries to gay and lesbian people. The principal speaker that year was to be the Episcopal bishop John Shelby Spong, who was a favorite target of the religious right wing. I agreed to lead a workshop on ethical issues. During the question period, when I took written questions, I was taken aback by one of them. Calling attention to how Christ is depicted by artists in different cultures in ways indigenous to those cultures, the questioner wondered whether it would be acceptable to depict Christ on the cross dressed in drag. (That is, a male dressed as a female.) As I stumbled over a reply to a totally unanticipated question, I remarked that while I didn't wish to stand in judgment of people who feel the need to dress in drag, my basic understanding was that this was a pathological behavior. I don't know that I would put it that way now, but that is what I said then. So it came as a shock to read in yet another IRD release that this Rainbow of Light Conference had featured the idea of Christ dressed in drag. Given the fact that the writer had been there and had apparently even tape-recorded the event, this was clearly dishonest—and also a good reflection of how the press can blow up trivia. Nevertheless, the story took on a life of its own throughout the Bible Belt. Months later I was still getting echoes of that initial account, some of which attributed the idea of Christ dressed in drag to Bishop Spong (who, to my knowledge, was utterly unaware of what had transpired in my workshop). The echoes came in the form of comments in conservative newspapers and a fair amount of what my secretary and I jokingly referred to as "Christian hate mail."

I have already referred to the departure of Robert and Elizabeth Dole from Foundry. That occasioned further attention from the press. In early 1995, the conservative *Washington Times* ran a gossip item noting that Elizabeth Dole had been present at Foundry when I had allegedly attacked the Republican "Contract with America" and dismissed the divinity of Christ. The source of these two misrepresentations was, again, the IRD. The *Washington Times* piece went on to wonder how the Doles could continue to attend such a church. I had been interviewed by telephone prior to the appearance of this little stinger, but that had made no difference. A few weeks later notice appeared through the Associated Press that the senator and his wife were shopping around for a different church. The story became national news, and I was interviewed by the Associated Press, the *Washington Post*, and the *New York Times*, among others. I formulated a brief written statement, which I read to journalists when they called, expressing my regard for the Doles who, I said, knew they were cordially welcomed by Foundry. I noted that church participation is a very personal decision and they would have to be the ones to speak about their own decision making.

Gus Niebuhr from the *New York Times* called to ask whether they were leaving Foundry, and I gave my standard response. The next day's *Times* reported that sources close to the Doles had confirmed that they were seeking another church. I took that to be definitive and that the "sources" might even have been the Doles themselves. A number of papers reported that the Doles considered the Foundry minister to be too liberal. Then, during the summer of 1995, Elizabeth Dole sent me a message to say that she would be uniting with another church the following day. I wrote that they would be in my prayers that day, and they were.

I didn't want to make a public issue of what really is a very personal decision, but to some degree they had already done so. Even though neither of them explained it to me in this way, I could see the awkwardness of their situation.

I did regret their decision. I thought the symbolism of both major party candidates for the presidency coming from the same church could have been a splendid reminder to the nation that there are some things that transcend political differences, and the Doles' decision had no discernible effect on the outcome of the 1996 election. In my nearly three years as their pastor we enjoyed friendly relations. And, while my political views did not always coincide with the senator's, I felt that he did want to be a force for good in American public life—and often succeeded. I have already mentioned how he teamed up with another Foundry member, Senator (and Ambassador) George McGovern in supporting an innovative global school lunch program, which saved this humanitarian effort from being perceived, and rejected, as a partisan move.[1]

Advice from Media Experts

As a result of experiences like this, I learned a few things about relating to the mass media. Some of that is simply the gift of experience, of learning the hard way. Part is learning not to be afraid. I have known church leaders, including even bishops and heads of denominations, who tend to shy away from the press. Sometimes that reflects a commendable modesty—

1. Speaking of symbolism, Foundry does have the distinction of being, at least for a time, one of the only churches in American history (if there have been any others) in which there were two defeated candidates for the presidency, one from each of the major parties—Senator McGovern in 1972 and Senator Dole in 1996.

not wanting to appear to be a publicity seeker; sometimes it shows mistrust of journalists and a fear that one will be misquoted. I understand that. Yet if one thinks of print and broadcast journalism as a vast expansion of one's audience, and if one has something to say, then perhaps we shouldn't be so reticent. The fact that there is so much coarseness and corruption in print and on the airwaves, along with a good deal of political and religious demagoguery, should increase our sense of responsibility. It is, in a broad sense, a very important mission field! I came to feel the full force of this during my Foundry years. I had many opportunities during those years to address this wider audience, and I rarely turned them down. I did, however, turn down invitations to participate in national Sunday morning talk shows, for my first responsibility was to the church, which was the heart of my ministry. I cannot imagine what I could have said on such talk shows that would have compensated for the loss of the integrating center of my ministry.

Of course, there are many temptations that accompany such attention, foremost among them a false sense of self-importance. I learned along the way that we pastors must concentrate on the message that we believe people need to hear. It is when we are most self-conscious that we are most likely to fall flat. I believe the first rule of relating to the media is akin to the first rule of preaching: Have something to say that is worth saying, and try not to get in the way!

When, after two or three years at Foundry, I started having to deal with serious controversy, I got some very good advice from three experts. One of these was Wesley Pippert, a loyal Foundry member. Wes headed the University of Missouri's graduate journalism program in Washington, and he had been a leading journalist with United Press International, including a stint as White House correspondent during the Carter years. He gave me two pieces of advice. First, he said, when interviewed by print journalists (newspapers or magazines), remember that the less you say the more likely they will quote what you say. That is, you will be in better control of the message you really want to convey if you provide less to quote. His second point was that when interviewed by broadcast journalists (radio or television), remember that you don't have to answer the question they ask you.

There is a lot to be said for both of those points, but I couldn't possibly follow either of those pieces of advice because, as a preacher and teacher, I've always wanted to *explain* everything! Unfortunately that can get you in real trouble: You wind up saying too much, which gives the journalist more to choose from. The art, practiced by most effective politicians, is to say the same thing in different words. I did follow the advice on one occasion, in the midst of the White House impeachment controversy, when a talented young reporter for a Midwestern newspaper was trying to draw me out on my pastoral conversations with the president. I didn't blame her for trying; that was her job. But as politely as I could I made clear that such conversations were privileged. I explained that I would want all of her readers to have increased confidence that their ministers, priests, or rabbis would respect things said in confidence. She readily agreed with that and went on to a couple of other questions. Then she found a way to rephrase her initial question. Again, I explained that I could not speak of such things. Of course, she agreed. But then, a few minutes later, there was an especially adroit rephrasing of the same question. And I replied as I had before that I couldn't go into that. Well, she said, you're just not going to answer that, are you? No, I replied. We both laughed. She wrote an unusually perceptive article, but without pushing the limit.

While I usually said too much to the print journalists, I eventually got better at refining the points I most wanted to get across. On a few occasions, such as in response to inquiries about the Doles leaving Foundry or, later, when asked whether I was to be one of President Clinton's three spiritual advisers, I could anticipate getting numbers of calls. It was possible simply not to respond at all, and there were times when I did not. But when taking such calls I found it useful to write out a brief statement from one or two quotable sentences and then repeat that, making sure the reporter got the words straight. Sometimes it was necessary to repeat the statement two or three times. To that extent, I was following Wes's advice.

I long resisted Wes's comment concerning interviews with broadcast journalists and pondered whether it is honest to avoid a reporter's questions by giving my answer to the question I think should have been asked. But I've concluded that the person being interviewed has every right to control what he or she is going to communicate to that great unseen audience. Sometimes an interviewer will have a theme, slant, or interpretation of the news that he or she is trying to put across, using the interviewee to do it. In this case, one may challenge a leading question that begins "Don't you think that . . . ?" or "Would you agree that . . . ?" I don't consider it dishonest to cut through that with what you really want to say to this audience. Incidentally, many of the national talk shows have advance people who call a prospective interviewee to size up whether this is the person they really want to put on the program. At that point honesty is called for. One should be very clear about what one may or may not have to contribute to the prospective discussion. We should turn down requests to be interviewed if we do not really have anything to say that we believe the unseen audience needs to hear. But if we do have something worth saying, we should go about saying it the best way we can, whether or not that accords with the interviewer's goals.

I learned one thing early on about the brief statements given by people interviewed on the evening news. The statements, often only eight or ten seconds long, will have been culled from an interview lasting a whole lot longer. On several occasions I was interviewed for as much as twenty minutes. Then, on the evening news program, only a few words were used. The news editors cannot be blamed for that since time is very limited, and in my experience the major evening news programs usually made their selections quite responsibly. I often felt that they had taken exactly the right quote—or at least that I was not being quoted out of context. But now, when I see a U.S. senator or even a foreign chief of state saying a few words, I assume that the actual conversation was much longer.

Another point of interest: On a number of the talk shows on, for example, MSNBC or Fox, the person being interviewed may be squirreled away in a small room, isolated from other human beings, facing the tiny lens of a camera, responding to questions from a remotely positioned interviewer (perhaps in another city). To the viewer, it can be made to appear that the interviewer and interviewee are seeing each other. The interviewer can usually see the person being interviewed, but that person sees only the camera. Carolyn pointed out to me that it is important to look straight into the lens and, if possible, to smile a bit.

Tom McAnally, who was chief press officer for United Methodist Communications for some years, was another source of wise counsel at a number of points. He gave me one piece of advice that I really needed to hear: Avoid expressing anger on camera. I am not exactly a quick-tempered person by nature, but I am quite capable of getting into the heat of an argument—especially when I think I'm right and other people are wrong. The frown, the tightened mouth, the raised voice, the flashing eyes—these don't go over well with a television audience. They probably don't go over very well with God either. "A soft answer turneth away wrath," as the Bible says. Since the heart of the message I usually want to get across is about the centrality of love, I've had to remind myself again and again that the message itself had better be delivered in a loving spirit. Such a spirit is ultimately a gift of God, but we must be open to receive and then express it.

I suppose there are times when a touch of indignation can convey the same thing, if it comes across as an appeal to the better values of the audience and if it is not accompanied by hate. But righteous indignation can so easily turn into self-righteousness, which is the direct antithesis of love.

Some of the most interesting press encounters I had were with Christian radio networks. Almost invariably they represented conservative evangelicalism, bordering on fundamentalism. At first, I resisted being interviewed by these programs. It seemed clear to me that the talk show hosts had read some of the right-wing caricatures of the church and me and that this was an opportunity to demonstrate to the audience of evangelical Christians just what kind of apostate preacher President Clinton was listening to from the pulpit. I was also a bit fearful that my words would be tape-recorded and then selectively used out of context. But after being assured that the programs would be live and not edited, I decided to take the risks, and I'm glad I did. I'm sure I am right about various talk show hosts having read the negative caricatures before the program, because the questions would be framed right out of those sources. But, anticipating that, I had chapter and verse right at hand in my office where I was being interviewed (by telephone). A misquote from one of my earlier books could easily be placed in its context, and I could explain it in understandable theological terms. In a few moments, the talk show host would loosen up and we would have a real conversation. I could sense and appeal to the basic goodwill of the usual Christian radio talk show host. Often there would be an opportunity to take questions phoned in to the studio, so I had an opportunity to interact directly with the conservative audience. Again, I often sensed a level of goodwill once we had gotten through the veil of misunderstanding. On several occasions I ended the conversation by asking the host if I could say one more thing to the audience. Of course, he would answer. I then proceeded to ask the listeners to pray for me in the midst of an unusually challenging ministry in the nation's capital. That was, of course, an altogether disarming request! Was it also a bit cynical? Perhaps only God knows the answer to that. But by this point in the conversation I really did think of the audience—at least many of them—as being fellow Christians in the better sense of the word. And that was one way to help them feel that too.

I disagree with the theological and political orientation of many evangelicals, but my main concern is with the self-righteousness and intolerance that can so often accompany Christian faith—both evangelical and more liberal forms of the faith. Conservatives and liberals need to learn how to speak to one another with mutual regard, and I discovered brief opportunities for doing that on Christian talk radio.

I also have to thank Amber Kahn for offering sound, and sometimes shrewd, advice. Amber was press officer for the Interfaith Alliance, of which I was a board member and for two years president, and had a sure sense of what kinds of media opportunities would be useful and what kinds risky. She gave me a better sense of the "map" of Washington, D.C., media and often provided valuable suggestions of how to approach particular journalists. I can also thank Dean Snyder, then communications director of our Baltimore-Washington Conference, for helpful assessments and advice. Experienced media advisers can help us pastors address the media with greater self-assurance, thereby extending our ministry beyond the bounds of the local parish we serve.

The Troubled State of American Media

After a few years of interacting with print and broadcast journalists, I began to form a few opinions about the current role of the media in American life. It is obviously very important, a pervasive aspect of our culture. Much about it is quite positive. I think of the extraordinary television documentaries that have drawn us vividly into aspects of our history and the world of nature. At its best, television introduces average American homes to knowledge and dramatic performances such as those in the PBS *Masterpiece Theatre* series; there are also excellent children's educational programs such as *Sesame Street.* Alongside such positive contributions of the media, however, there are negatives: A good deal of television programming is coarse and sleazy. You don't have to be a fundamentalist to deplore the intrusions of cheap sex and unrestrained violence into our homes via television. And I hope it doesn't seem unduly elitist to criticize the dumbing down of America through many of the standard sitcoms.

My main media contacts, however, were not with the entertainment aspects of the media but with the news and commentary. Here too I can record some positive experiences. Along the way I had the privilege of being interviewed by very thoughtful journalists. It is to the credit of their news organizations that they are supported and encouraged in their work.

On the whole, though, I regret what seems to be the increasing tendency of news organizations (print and broadcast) to go for sensationalism and to look for and exaggerate conflict. We need to ask why this is. My guess is that the media are responding to ever increasing competition. Early in the twentieth century the term *yellow journalism* described the results of cutthroat competition among daily newspapers. Most cities of any size had several competing newspapers. To sell papers, one had to be first with the news, and one had to exploit the most sensational stories. William Randolph Hearst and others made fortunes out of news empires by appealing to the lower instincts of a mass public. Over time, there was a winnowing out of unsuccessful newspapers. Competition began to disappear, even in major cities. When I first came to the Washington, D.C., area in 1966 there were three fairly strong newspapers, two of which I considered to be very good. Gradually the *Washington Post* took over the whole market, joined a few years ago by the still-not-so-consequential *Washington Times* (which has been heavily subsidized by the Unification Church network of Rev. Sun Myung Moon). Meanwhile, the three giants in television—NBC, CBS, and ABC—enjoyed a near monopoly for years, with their respective evening news audiences numbering a substantial percentage of the American public.

What has changed? Technology has brought a return of cutthroat competition. Television is no longer limited to a handful of publicly allocated channels. Now by virtue of cable and satellite technologies, even homes in remote locations have access to scores of channels with competing programming. Even the giants now must compete aggressively for audience share. Similarly, new print technologies have encouraged publication of many more magazines, and most parts of the country have access to several newspapers—not local, but national. Newspapers such as the *New York Times*, the *Wall Street Journal*, the *Christian Science Monitor*, the *Washington Post*, *USA Today*, and the *Los Angeles Times* can now be downloaded, printed, and distributed in many locations. Indeed, many newspapers are easily and cheaply available online at one's own computer. The effects of increased competition are discernible in a gradual return of sensationalism as news organizations seek to increase their share of the mass market. I'm not sure what I would prescribe to deal with this—certainly we do not want to return to small media monopolies and retreat from the technological advances. But thoughtful people need to do all they can to encourage and support higher standards of quality. And, as I noted before, that means we do not retreat from opportunities to participate directly.

I came to see where some of the professional challenges lie for journalists. Most reporters and commentators are not narrow specialists; they cannot be real experts on all the things they cover. Therefore, they must struggle to understand what is really going on and then find ways to communicate that to a public that knows even less than they do. Invariably this means seeking out the event or statement or picture that best conveys the larger reality. A sloppy journalist—or one with an ax to grind—may emphasize a small part of the larger picture that really does not represent the whole. I recall one of the huge antiwar demonstrations during the Vietnam War. About half a million people assembled on the Mall next to the Washington Monument in a quite peaceful, civil assemblage. Many of the people carried small American flags to demonstrate their underlying loyalty to their country. But in covering the event, the media focused not on the half million loyal Americans but on thirty or forty members of the "Weather Underground," who conveyed an almost violent militancy. Thus, the media conveyed the impression that this whole demonstration was made up of people who hated their country. Such journalistic dishonesty can be communicated by a selectively chosen photograph, the focus of a TV camera, or an isolated interview with somebody who doesn't really represent the whole picture. Of course, no journalist can tell it all. But a serious journalist strives for the image, the anecdote, the quotation, the picture that somehow captures the essence of the story. In my own encounters with the media, I ran into both kinds of journalists. I devoutly hope that the pressures of journalistic competition in our time do not make it ever more difficult for the great reporters and commentators to function.

Collectively the churches of America also reach a very large "audience" made up of tens of millions of people. It seems to me that we have a responsibility to help that very large segment of the public be more discerning in its approach to the media, encouraging the best and criticizing (and not patronizing) the parts that are unworthy of the values of truth and goodness by which we strive to live.

Chapter Ten

Crisis in the White House

In which I am drawn into a major presidential crisis—struggle with special responsibilities of the pastoral role and a continuing role as social ethicist—am asked to serve as one of the president's spiritual advisers—encounter new kinds of press scrutiny—write a small book in the midst of the crisis and reflect on the propriety of that—take some criticism—engage in debates—reflect in new ways on the relationship between personal character and public responsibility

When I looked at the front page of the *Washington Post* on Wednesday, January 21, 1998, I knew there was trouble ahead—for the country, for our church, and possibly for me personally. A headline story announced that special prosecutor Kenneth Starr was investigating evidence that President Clinton had lied under oath and committed an obstruction of justice. Compounding the legal issues was the underlying moral issue of his alleged sexual improprieties. The situation, details, and resolution are now a familiar chapter in American history. At the time it was evident that the Clinton presidency itself was at risk. The media grabbed hold of the story with bold headlines and breathless revelations of every sort. No lead or rumor was left unreported. News anchors of the major networks, then in Cuba to cover the pope's unprecedented visit there, rushed back to manage the sensational new story. Prognosticators, such as ABC's Sam Donaldson, were predicting that the president would shortly be forced to resign. And I was his pastor!

Over the next few days I was involved in a swirl of regular activity, much of it unrelated to the emerging presidential crisis. There were a number of pastoral counseling sessions, an adult education class, several committee meetings, a consultation on a lawsuit regarding the Boy Scouts' anti-gay policies, a PBS interview, and I was also part of a religious delegation that met with Yasir Arafat.[1]

Such things consumed most of that fateful week. As I looked toward Sunday my sermon hadn't yet jelled. It was to be the second in a series on aspects of Christian faith. In my long-range plan, this was to be a sermon in which I explored issues of biblical scholarship and interpretation—much needed in a time of polarization around issues of biblical authority. Now, in light of the exploding crisis, I couldn't imagine engaging the congregation in what would largely be an intellectual exercise about the Bible. Their spiritual need was going to be at a deeper level, especially in *this* congregation, which included the president. Should I simply abandon the announced topic and do something different?

I hadn't quite decided what to preach on by Saturday, when I was committed to go to Chicago for a consultation on—of all things—religion and politics. I took my laptop along to work on the sermon on the flights out and back.

At the Chicago meeting the presidential crisis was specifically, and wisely, excluded from our more theoretical discussion of issues. But, of course, during the breaks for coffee and lunch, that was the only thing anybody wanted to talk about. It was well known that I was pastor of the president's church, so I had to deal with a variety of questions and suggestions. I hardly knew what to say when I was privately singled out by two nationally prominent, though retired, leaders of the president's party. As his pastor, they told me, I might be one of the very few who should be prepared to tell the president that—for the sake of his party and his own healing—it was time for him to step down. I have not had occasion to talk with either of those people since; quite possibly both have, by now, changed their minds about the situation. I offer this now as an illustration of the climate bordering on hysteria of those days. Their comments deeply troubled me.

On the way back to Chicago's Midway Airport, the taxi's radio was full of the latest rumors and revelations and conjectures of how long before the

1. The Palestinian leader was in Washington to meet with President Clinton, and those conversations had gotten sidetracked by the presidential crisis—which Arafat must have found mystifying. He was also affected by some kind of flu bug, and he looked old and tired. In the meeting I asked him whether he and the Palestinians were willing to affirm the continued existence of Israel unequivocally, and he replied yes, they already had. I have strongly supported the national aspirations of the Palestinian people, although it seemed to me then—and still does—that both sides share responsibility for the continuing impasse. I didn't sense that Arafat had grasped that point.

president would have to resign. My stress level was rising. I certainly wasn't about to follow the advice I'd been given, at least not without clearer evidence that the president should take such a drastic step or that I, as a pastor, should advise it. There are times when a pastor must offer a hard prophetic word, but not as a response to hysteria in the media. We are, I reflected, called not only to be courageous but also to be wise. I felt it would be presumptuous to leap heavy-handedly into this high-stakes situation.

But what was I to say to the congregation the next day? I finally realized that the sermon title was *exactly* right for this occasion: "Taking the Bible Seriously." How better to take the Bible seriously than to search out some biblical wisdom that would be pertinent to the crisis. So that is the course I took.[2] Among other things, I spoke of how Isaiah 40 addressed the great trauma of Hebrew history, the Babylonian exile. I concluded the sermon by reading 1 Corinthians 13, Paul's wonderful essay on love, in its entirety. I said that is what I would read to the whole nation if I had an opportunity because I felt that was the word of grace the country most needed to hear. The wish was almost fulfilled, for an Associated Press reporter was present in the service, and in an article that appeared all over the country the next day, he quoted several verses of the Corinthians passage verbatim. People were generous in their response when they greeted me after the service, except for one steely eyed woman who earlier had participated in a hostile demonstration outside the church. "That," she pronounced concerning my sermon, "is the worst drivel I have ever heard." On sober reflection, I had to conclude that she was probably right. Even the best we can say must be, in the sight of God, little more than drivel. But, God be praised, even our drivel is sometimes used toward good ends. In this case it may have been to help calm people down while encouraging them to reflect on the crisis in light of our shared faith.

The Clintons were themselves present for the service. I chose this time to appear with them at the entrance to the church, where reporters and cameras were always in abundance when the first family was in attendance. I wanted to lend a visible kind of pastoral support. We had opportunity for a few words about the crisis. To my surprise, the picture of that scene appeared on the front page of the *New York Times* and other papers across the country. While this too might have been an example of overreporting, at least it conveyed an image balancing the negatives then flooding the press.

2. I have written more about this and have published the actual sermon in my *Speaking the Truth in Love* (Louisville, Ky.: Westminster John Knox Press, 1998).

My Skepticism—and Disappointment

In succeeding months the Starr investigation proceeded relentlessly, but the president affirmed his innocence on national television. He gave a generally well-received State of the Union message. He was supported by his own cabinet members, who accepted the denials, and he proceeded with the nation's business. Increasingly I was interviewed by the media, often as a counter to conservative religious figures such as Jerry Falwell who were calling for the president's resignation or impeachment. I was not in a position to know for sure, but there was enough about the charges that did not ring true to lead me to be skeptical about the whole package. I generally accepted requests for interviews because I did not want the media coverage of the story to be dominated primarily by the negatives and, specifically, I did not want the impression to be left that religious leaders were united in condemning the president. When interviewed, I usually said that I would be disappointed to learn that the allegations were true, but that I was skeptical about them, and I could, with good conscience, continue to affirm much about this man and his leadership.

The crisis was reignited in midsummer of 1998 with Monica Lewinsky's testimony to the grand jury. The president agreed to be questioned by the grand jury on August 17. I participated in a Jesse Jackson television program on CNN the day before the president's testimony, which led to news coverage the next morning, the day of the president's scheduled testimony. Later that evening, obviously tired and under stress, President Clinton addressed the nation with a brief statement in which he acknowledged wrongdoing. The statement was, I thought, fairly clear. But over the next few days he was widely criticized in the press for not being apologetic enough and for criticizing the special prosecutor.

For me, both as a pastor and as a friend, the confirmation of his wrongdoing came as a real disappointment. Pastors face and deal with the whole range of human behaviors and attitudes. We confront both the negative and the positive aspects of human nature, in both ourselves and others, so we are not overwhelmingly surprised by anything. But we can be disappointed, and I was. The president made no effort, either publicly or privately, to hide the fact that he was disappointed in himself. We talked about that. In one phone conversation during the period when he was being criticized for not being sorry enough, he encouraged me to speak publicly of his remorse over his behavior. I did so during a televised "town meeting" on MSNBC where the president was again being taken to task for not apologizing sufficiently. Howard Fineman of *Newsweek*, who was also on the program, criticized me personally for allowing myself to be used by the president. Other panelists came to my rescue, but I wanted to reply directly. Perhaps I *was* being "used," I acknowledged, but I did not object, for I was being used by the president to reëmphasize his contrition, and I could see no problem with that! At no point, then or later, did he ever ask me to *condone* his behavior, which I could never have done. On the other hand, it surely was my sacred responsibility as pastor to encourage him to seek and find forgiveness and to understand afresh that by God's grace he could recover and grow spiritually. Several of us were encouraging him to make use of an upcoming White House prayer breakfast, when he would be meeting with a cross section of religious leaders, to make a fuller personal statement.

During this period several of his religious critics called attention to the biblical account of King David's deplorable acts toward Bathsheba and her husband. David had directly ordered the death of a loyal soldier in order to cover up his own adultery with the soldier's wife, the beautiful Bathsheba. The courageous prophet Nathan confronted the king directly, forcing him to repent. In recounting this story, such critics as Jerry Falwell emphasized the judgment upon David and, not so incidentally, questioned whether some of us who were ministering to the president shouldn't be Nathans to his David. Should we not "speak truth to power"?

In some respects this was indeed that kind of situation, and there may have been more communication on that level than Falwell and others imagined. (The president didn't need a Nathan at this point to explain that what he had done was wrong. He was well enough aware of that, as was the whole country.) But reflecting on the David and Bathsheba story as a parallel to the Clinton situation, I had to remember two very important points. In the first place, bad as it was, the president's misbehavior wasn't on the same level as David's unspeakable act. And in the second place David, having sought the Lord's forgiveness, received it and retained his crown. He was to be remembered for the next thousand years and more as Israel's greatest king. Even Jesus, often referred to in the gospels as "Son of David," spoke of the great king in only positive terms. So the David story, tragic though it was, is largely about how it is possible to find forgiveness and restoration.

The Prayer Breakfast

The White House prayer breakfast was an annual event, held usually sometime in September. I had attended several of these in earlier years and planned to attend this one too. Prayer breakfasts are a frequent part of the Washington scene. I'm not sure they are well named; there usually isn't much "waiting on the Lord." Generally there is some prayer—perhaps at the beginning and end—but for the most part the occasions are times for discussion of issues of common concern. Sometimes they give more the appearance of civil religion, bringing to mind the well-spoken words of the prophet Amos about solemn religious festivals: "I hate, I despise your festivals, and I take no delight in your solemn assemblies. . . . But let justice roll down like waters, and righteousness like an everflowing stream" (Amos 5:21, 24). Speeches can entail some mixture of personal witnessing with commentary on selected national issues. There is usually good conversation and always good food. I don't wish to be dismissive of these events; they are at least a reminder that there are values that transcend personal ambition and partisan conflict.

The Clintons always included representatives of different faiths, moving beyond Christianity and Judaism to involve Hindus, Muslims, and Buddhists as well as lesser-known faith communities. Even some of the president's arch-critics were invited, although they rarely came. I was delighted to meet people of faith traditions very different from my own and often surprised at how we could come to appreciate one another even in our disagreements. Typically the gathering would open with a welcome, often from Hillary Rodham Clinton, then a prayer by a religious leader. Following breakfast and informal conversation, President Clinton would speak to issues of the day, generally highlighting those that would involve the most important ethical concerns of the religious leaders. His grasp of issues was always impressive. Usually he would have a speech in hand that might have been prepared by one of the White House speechwriters, but he would typically put that aside to speak extemporaneously. Following the speech there was opportunity for open-ended questions and his responses, generally off the record.

Usually the events were held in the State Dining Room with perhaps a hundred or so people seated around tables of eight. In 1998, however, the event was moved to the East Room in order to accommodate two or three dozen more. In light of the presidential crisis, this was going to be far more important than the usual prayer breakfast. And this time the press, including television, would be invited to cover the president's remarks.

I had had a bit of a warm-up for the emotions of the day. Earlier in the morning I had appeared on the *Today* show with Rev. Paige Patterson, then president of the Southern Baptist Convention. Rev. Patterson was calling for the immediate resignation of the president. I countered that the nation would never find healing in this crisis with a loveless spirit and that we should be speaking the language of repentance and forgiveness. I'm sure neither of us convinced the other, and who knows which of us was more persuasive to the unseen audience.

At the White House, the air was electric with anticipation and, in my case, with apprehension. I knew the president was going to offer a much more complete statement of repentance than he had previously. I wasn't sure what he would encounter with the religious leaders, most of whom had not been invited on the basis of their known support for the president in this time of crisis. In fact, I had learned that the head of one denomination was seriously contemplating openly calling for the president's resignation. Anybody there could have gathered headlines unto himself or herself by doing that and then speaking to the press afterward. Several other members of the administration were present, including Vice President Gore (who introduced the president) and several cabinet members. White House staff members acted as host or hostess at each of the tables, and they seemed a bit nervous as well.

President Clinton had spent much of the night struggling with what he was going to say. What came out was a very heartfelt statement of his contrition and the remorse he felt at what he had done to his family and friends and the nation. He offered no excuses and no criticism of the special prosecutor who had been investigating him for years. Then he went further. In this situation, he acknowledged, it was probably a good thing that he had been forced to face up to his serious need to change. Toward the end of his statement, President Clinton spoke of his need to have spiritual counselors at hand to whom he would be accountable. Without naming them specifically, he indicated that he had asked three people to serve in this way in the months ahead.

His speech came before breakfast, and he had planned to take questions after we had eaten. But during breakfast, first one person, then another and another went up to him to voice their personal affection and prayers for his healing. There was a good deal of emotion. These personal moments wound up preempting the planned question period. As far as I could tell, there wasn't anybody present who had not been moved by his comments, nor was there much cynicism about it. In the end, my fears about the occasion proved groundless. If anybody had in fact planned to use the occasion for public criticism, that did not happen. I suspect that most if not all of the leaders of different faith communities found his words of contrition to be spiritually authentic.

The Spiritual Advisers

At the prayer breakfast the president had spoken of his designation of three spiritual advisers but hadn't named them. I already knew, however. He had called me a few days earlier, asking whether I could be one of three or four spiritual advisers who could help him understand and deal with his problem and to help ensure that his misbehavior would not happen again. After discussing the matter with him, I agreed to serve. The other two advisers were the well-known minister and religious writer Dr. Tony Campolo and the Rev. Gordon MacDonald, a prominent evangelical pastor who had dealt with similar issues in his own life. Following the breakfast, the three of us began to plan the approach we would take. We agreed that this would not be an exercise of what psychologists call "enabling." In other words, we would not condone or find excuses for the president's misbehavior, any more than he had done in his statement at the prayer breakfast. Instead, we would take the president at his word—that he really wanted to find healing and to move on. We would do all we could to help him, both for his sake and for the sake of the country.

Soon enough the press learned who we were, although I refused to say anything about my own role until an enterprising *Washington Post* reporter confirmed it with the White House. Subsequently I made clear that these interactions were personal and confidential. We all had a difficult problem here. On the one hand, spiritual counseling really does have to be confidential. On the other hand, it was important for the people of this country to know that their president was doing something about his obvious moral breakdown. I don't fault him for letting it be known that he was receiving this kind of spiritual counseling and that he was keeping faith with the process in the weeks and months ahead.

The basic plan was that the three of us would try to meet with him as a group to establish some mutual understandings about the process, and then we would take turns, week by week, in speaking to him individually. The Oval Office staff was fully cooperative; the environment was structured in ways that would reinforce his good intentions. It did not prove possible to schedule the one-on-one sessions every single week, but the president honored his commitment and met with us with great regularity until the end of his second term of office in January 2001.

When it became known that we were the ones working with the president in this way, two or three psychologists and psychiatrists privately volunteered their professional assessments and, implicitly, their services.

I could understand this in human terms, but it continues to seem odd to me that a professional would venture a diagnosis without even talking with the person in question. I am not a trained psychologist, but I have to say that I thought their various assessments were off base. The experience as a whole reinforced in my mind the recognition that, while competent psychological therapy is also often invaluable, pastoral counseling at a more spiritual level can sometimes touch the human heart at a very deep level.

How effective this spiritual counseling arrangement was in the long run I cannot claim to know. My intuition was that it was helpful at several levels. Quite apart from President Clinton's own special need, I think such a regular time for spiritual counsel would be valuable for any president. The presidency can be a lonely post, even though a president is surrounded by clamoring people and constant pressures. Times for quiet reflection with two or three trusted spiritual advisers can help reinforce a president's deeper values and sense of the transcendent grace of God by which he (and someday she) is held. President Clinton voiced his appreciation publicly on several occasions, and I note with appreciation that, at least to my knowledge, there was never again the kind of moral breakdown that had caused the crisis. I attribute that mostly to his family and his own resolve, which it was our responsibility to reinforce in whatever way we could.

The Book

In late August, prior to the prayer breakfast, I was approached by my publisher, Westminster John Knox Press, the book publishing division of the Presbyterian Publishing Corporation. Would I be interested in writing a small book on the presidential crisis that could be published quickly as a contribution to the national debate? I had to pause over that! I had written a number of books over the years, mostly on Christian ethics and social issues. The presidential crisis bristled with ethical issues, a challenge to a Christian ethicist like myself. At the same time, however, I was also closely involved as a pastor to the president. Would it be proper to write a book about a situation I would view not only as an ethicist but also as pastor? Even if I thought it would be appropriate for me to make such a contribution, what would it look like to others? It could be a potential minefield. And, appearances aside, I wondered if I had at that point thought the situation through to the point where I would have things to say that needed to be said. I asked the publisher, Davis Perkins, whether I could reflect on his proposal, for I thought the upcoming prayer breakfast might help clarify my thinking. Moreover, the Starr Report had not yet appeared, and I wanted to see what was in it and how it was received. We left it at that.

Following the prayer breakfast and the appearance of the Starr Report (which, as a bizarre coincidence, became public in lurid detail the very day of the breakfast), the situation became clearer. I felt I did have things to say, centering on the great contrast between the vindictive tone of the report and the themes of grace and redemption that are closer to the heart of my own faith and, I believe, to the deeper values widely shared in this country. I was ready to write the book. It had to be fairly short and it had to be written quickly if it was going to have any effect on the public conversation. I wrote a first draft in three or four weeks, interacting along the way with a gifted Westminster John Knox editor, Stephanie Egnotovich. My clergy colleague Walter Shropshire and members of my family and a handful of other people offered helpful suggestions, and the book was published. The title itself went through several versions, but we agreed to *From the Eye of the Storm*, my working title from the start. The publishers wanted the subtitle *The President's Pastor Speaks Out*. That didn't seem quite right to me. Yes, I was pastor to the president, but so were several others, including the other two designated spiritual advisers, Tony Campolo and Gordon MacDonald. We finally settled on *A Pastor to the President Speaks Out*.

My family and I had decided that it would be wrong to accept any royalties from book sales for personal use, so all the royalties went to charitable causes (which included the church and several nonprofit organizations). While President Clinton himself had not asked me to write the book, I made him aware of it and sought and received his permission to quote from a couple of our personal interactions. I was clear that there must be no violation of my pastoral commitment to preserve confidentiality.

I had hoped, of course, that the book would find a very wide readership, but, alas, that was not to be! It sold about nine thousand copies, but definitely not tens or hundreds of thousands! A vast majority of my fellow citizens somehow escaped reading the book, and it seemed to escape the attention of the Pulitzer Prize committee! It did, however, open up many media opportunities for me to comment on the presidential crisis, including C-Span coverage of the press conference at which the book was launched in late 1998, appearances on a number of national network programs, and feature stories in several widely circulated newspapers. The response to the book also included some highly critical comments from those who disagreed with what I had to say or even with my right to say anything at all in book form. So, for good or ill, the book provided access to the national conversation.

I sought in the book to emphasize the importance of the cardinal virtue of love in resolving the crisis. I definitely did not mean a fuzzy "anything goes" conception of love, and yet love is prior to any other virtue. It is the virtue without which there can be no other virtue, for in the absence of love the practice of other virtues can be mean-spirited, self-centered, or moralistic.[3] It had become clear, I thought, that the essence of the president's wrongdoing was a disconnection between sex and love.[4] But that flaw is characteristic of a good deal of American culture in our time. Is it possible, I asked, to address such a failure of love in an unloving way, as we were being invited to by the highly moralistic and legalistic attitudes of the special prosecutor's office and Clinton's critics in Congress and the media? We are reminded of Jesus' question to those wanting to stone the woman caught in adultery: Which of you will cast the first stone? Would stoning the woman to death (as required by an earlier Hebrew law) have improved the morality of her community? I wondered whether treating the president harshly would have healed the nation's moral weakness.

This theme led, of course, to a consideration of repentance and forgiveness, to a discussion of private versus public expressions of morality, and to other issues. There was no need in any of this discussion to mount a defense of the president's behavior, either his sexual misbehavior or his misleading the American people about it. I couldn't have defended any of that, and I'm sure he wouldn't have wanted me to. He had acknowledged the sinfulness. Now the question was what the consequences should be and whether he could be forgiven. I also raised ethical issues related to the investigation: To what extent was it politically motivated? Had he been set up prior to his original testimony in January 1998? Did it matter that Linda Tripp had exploited and betrayed a friendship by secretly recording her conversations with Monica Lewinsky? It all seemed the stuff of soap operas, but the importance of these issues for our national life could scarcely have been more clear.

3. William J. Bennett went after President Clinton in his book *The Death of Outrage* (New York: Free Press, 1998). The highly moralistic tone of that book struck me as missing this central virtue altogether. But love is often misunderstood by those who yearn for objective guidelines that give priority to correctness over caring. To paraphrase the language of a Broadway musical, it is possible to be so full of being right that we can't be good.

4. A conversation at the time with my bishop, Felton Edwin May, was especially helpful in clarifying this point and its implications.

My own assessment was that President Clinton had indeed been set up and that the prosecutorial process was indefensible.[5] No other president had ever undergone quite so relentless a scrutiny. Still, his own acknowledged actions had made it easy for his adversaries. The question finally before Congress and the nation was what the consequences should be. One heard it said (by many ordinary people as well as journalists and political adversaries) that regardless of what one might think of the methods by which his conduct had been exposed, a president could not be allowed to "get away with it." A prominent Republican congressman, later part of the House of Representatives prosecution team, made the point to me in almost exactly those words. They struck me as odd. Of course one shouldn't be able to get away with such things. But who could say that he had? He had already suffered very serious consequences, both personally and politically. Occasionally during those months I would be asked what we should say to our children and youth. Had an example been set before them of wrong conduct that would lead them to follow that path? That might be a hard question to assess, but surely nobody could conclude that the episode showed that the conduct didn't matter. The president and his family had gone through a whole lot of suffering. Should there have been additional consequences?

Former president Gerald Ford suggested that the president should be required to face the Congress in a televised event in which a "harshly worded rebuke" was rendered by members of both parties. That would register the judgment of the people unmistakably, but it would have been the kind of "cleansing" event that would permit president and people to put the sorry chapter behind them and proceed afresh about the nation's business. At the time, I thought that something of that sort made sense. In my book I compared this kind of thing with the "tough love" expressed when family and friends gather to confront an alcoholic loved one and to set forth a path toward recovery. In hindsight, however, I do not regret the failure of Congress to move in that direction, for in light of all the circumstances—including the sexual misbehavior of some of the leaders of

5. Since then two books have carefully examined the undercover efforts to bring the president down, although enough had already been publicly aired to make the point—to me and to a very large number of my fellow citizens. David Brock's *Blinded by the Right* (New York: Crown Publishers, 2002) expresses the author's remorse over the important and dishonest role he had played in this drama. Joe Conason and Gene Lyons, *The Hunting of the President* (New York: St. Martin's Press, 2000) documents what the book's subtitle refers to as the ten-year campaign to destroy Bill and Hillary Clinton.

Congress and their own misleading of the public—it would perhaps have been too hypocritical. Perhaps it is best that things worked out as they did.

Amid all the condemnation the president was taking, including self-condemnation, it also seemed to me that some people were overlooking very positive aspects of his moral character. I wrote, and still believe, that

> many Americans believe Bill Clinton has been a good President, a fine leader. Many things have gone well on his "watch." He has been gifted in the arts of reconciliation, and he has grown immensely in his grasp of the problems of the nation and the world. Such gifts are not to be squandered, either by him or by the nation. Among his gifts has been a striking resiliency. He has, in his political career, suffered serious setbacks, but he has always recovered with grace and good humor. I believe his resiliency has spiritual roots.[6]

It is not a part of a pastor's job description to make final judgments about the character of others; that is in God's hands. God alone knows the depths of the human heart. Yet such things as devotion to the public good and sensitivity to those who have been marginalized are also marks of moral character. We are all flawed. Surely we do not finally have to be defined by our flaws alone. In the book I commented that, while all forms of sin are harmful, I believe that sins of weakness are less damaging than sins of malice. Bill Clinton never seemed to me to be a hater. His point of weakness was well publicized, but he was a whole lot more than that. My personal interactions reinforced my appreciation for him as a person.

Pastors often find themselves in situations where they must make judgments, but there is an important distinction between judgment and judgmentalism. Human beings are multifaceted, a strange, sometimes unpredictable mixture of sin and moral goodness. We can best help people overcome sinful flaws if we allow ourselves to be channels of God's grace, reminding them of their worth as children of God and of their opportunities to grow.

Between Impeachment and Acquittal

President Clinton was impeached by the House of Representatives in a largely party-line vote on Saturday, December 19, 1998.

6. J. Philip Wogaman, *From the Eye of the Storm: A Pastor to the President Speaks Out* (Louisville, Ky.: Westminster John Knox Press, 1998), 136.

By coincidence, I was scheduled to preach at the Washington National Cathedral the following day. This was the last Sunday of Advent, and I was to preach on the lectionary texts for that day. Both the Isaiah and the Matthew passages emphasized the coming birth of one who would be called Immanuel, which means "God with us." After developing the theme in the sermon, I asked how we could really believe that God is with us at times of personal and national crisis. I concluded that

> those words do not define the weakness of our faith, but its strength. For the one we know as the infant in the manger was to become, on the cross, the one who gave everything for us. He is the one who is present to us in all the hurt and evil the world can throw at us. He is that deep grace we experience in all of our wretchedness, to lift us up and make us whole. God is with us.

In his letter of invitation the preceding summer, Dean Nathan Baxter of the cathedral had urged me to address some theme "of national import." Little could either of us have known back then what would be stirring that weekend. I could not ignore what had happened the very day before "of national import." So I spoke of the destructive partisanship of the past decade, quoting an eloquent passage from an article by Dan Balz in the previous day's *Washington Post:*

> A decade of destructive partisanship, personal attack and win-at-all-cost politics has crystalized in Washington this week, and the question no one can begin to answer is where it will end. The extraordinary events of the past 48 hours suggest that the simple civilities that once helped to lubricate the rough game of politics are being swept away.[7]

I acknowledged the despair most of us feel amid public mean-spiritedness. Our nation stood in need of great moral renewal. Yet, I said, "moral renewal cannot come on the back of a vindictive spirit. Moral renewal can only rise on the wings of love!" Should the president now be removed from office? I continued:

> I cannot and do not believe so. I believe it would be a great tragedy. Others may disagree. All of us should acknowledge that we could be

7. Dan Balz, "One Week Defines Partisan," *Washington Post,* December 18, 1998.

> wrong. But upon this we must agree: Love is not a soft and useless virtue; it is the virtue without which there is no other virtue. The God who is Immanuel to us is love to us, and it is this Immanuel who alone can see us through . . . perhaps in ways none of us can quite imagine.

And so it went. As I look back on those months, it seems that God was seeing us through, despite our clumsy imperfections. I often found myself addressing the vast media audience afforded by print, radio, and television. Sometimes it seemed to go well, sometimes not so well. My little book, which appeared in early December, was partly responsible for the media attention. The book was launched with a press conference at the National Press Club. Since that day in early December was a slow period for the news, the press conference was covered live by C-Span and preceded by interviews on a couple of network morning shows. I still wince over my foolishness at one of those. A publicist had suggested that I use the occasion to plug the book, so I held it up two or three times for the TV audience—for which I was properly rebuked by a Foundry member. Other occasions went better. My favorite, which probably did not reach a very large audience, was an hour-long interview by a perceptive Seventh Day Adventist on an Adventist radio hook-up. He had read the book, understood what I was trying to say, then drew me out about the deeper theological and practical implications.

During the period after the impeachment, I was also drawn into some out-and-out debates. I'm probably not very good at that, but I confess to a certain enjoyment of the matching of wits, even though I'm sure it brings out the worst in my character! Three or four of these debates were occasioned by the nearly simultaneous publication of my book and a volume with contrasting views. The latter, *Judgment Day at the White House*,[8] also dealt with the presidential crisis and featured a harsh public declaration that had been signed by a group of ethicists. While a handful of the essays in the book were critical of the declaration, most spoke bitingly of the president's behavior and of the September prayer breakfast attendees who had, in their judgment, been too quick to forgive. One essay even questioned whether a nation *can* forgive, which I found to be an extraordinary conclusion in light of the well-exercised power of executive pardon (where a governor or president acts in behalf of a state or nation) and such impressive illustrations as the famous South African

8. Gabriel Fackre, ed., *Judgment Day at the White House* (Grand Rapids: Wm. B. Eerdmans Publishing Co., 1999).

Truth and Reconciliation Commission. I was invited to debate formulators of the declaration whose work appeared in the book. One of these debates was before a large crowd at the annual meeting of the American Academy of Religion, where it seemed obvious that a clear majority of those scholars were not about to join in the condemnation of the president, and another was at Fourth Presbyterian Church in Chicago. I doubt, however, that anybody's mind was changed by either of these public debates. Yet another debate occurred on Ted Koppel's *Nightline* program on ABC.

In some respects, the debate that mattered least of all was the one I enjoyed most. It was before a group made up mostly of conservative journalists and sponsored by the conservative Center for Religion and Ethics. The time of that debate turned out to be the very day on which the Senate finally voted on the articles of impeachment. While eating lunch at the center's offices and waiting for the debate, I watched the Senate vote on television. The well-known result was President Clinton's acquittal on both counts. So it was over. Within a minute or two of the last vote somebody came into the room where I was watching the Senate proceedings to tell me that my son Stephen was on the phone from Louisville, Kentucky. "Dad," he announced excitedly, "you have a new granddaughter." Our granddaughter Emily had just been born! So I began my part of the debate by a word of celebration: I had a new granddaughter!

It had been widely supposed by his critics that President Clinton would greet his acquittal with jubilation and gloating. I knew better. We had discussed this. He was a bright enough politician to know that celebration would be foolish. And he also continued to carry a deep sense of remorse for what he had done. His statement was brief, utterly without vindictiveness.

But it was over now. How would this president and this country fare in the future?

When asked from time to time about that, I said that I knew there were many who were disappointed by the acquittal of the president. Nevertheless, I trusted that he would conduct himself in such a way for the rest of his term that in the end even those who had wanted him to be removed from office would be glad that he was not. In the case of many, that was but wishful thinking. Yet, far from being immobilized by what had happened, he responded with his usual resiliency and continued to function and to grow in his presidency. Our spiritual advisory team continued to meet with him throughout the remainder of his term. The next year's White House prayer breakfast was a time for further healing.

Personal Character and Public Responsibility

Quite apart from the pastoral dimension of the impeachment crisis, I was challenged as a Christian ethicist to reflect on the relationship between personal character and public responsibility. Those who most condemned the president emphasized the importance of personal character. Flawed personal character impacts everything else, they said. On the other side, some (but by no means all) of his defenders appeared to believe that a political leader's personal life is of no public consequence. The only thing that matters, they argued, is his or her public leadership.

It seems to me that both views were partly right but largely wrong. Personal character is important for everybody, and it does affect all aspects of our lives. At the same time, in the public sphere it is the leadership and vision of a public official that counts most. Clearly there is some relationship between the two.

Nevertheless, nobody is perfect, and some of our easy assumptions can be very wrong. Have we not known public officials with severe personal flaws who, at the same time, gave extraordinary, even self-sacrificial service to others? And have we not known those who, while seemingly living exemplary lives at the personal level, provided deplorable leadership? In the latter category I would unhesitatingly classify some of the staunch supporters of racial segregation in, for example, the Senate, who were never touched by scandal in their personal lives. And in the former category, I think of a California legislative leader I knew some years ago who, while his personal life was troubled, still provided extraordinary leadership in the struggle against racial segregation and authored visionary mental health legislation. Sometimes our easy moralisms prove to be off the mark.

The problem may be that we have too narrow an understanding of personal character, often limiting it to things like sexual behavior. But isn't selfless devotion to the public good also an aspect of personal character in a politician? Thus, to get at the personal character of our president—as some were so eager to do—did we not have to factor in his extraordinary empathy for marginalized people and his deep vocational commitment to public service? I would just as soon not get into the business of evaluating the personal character of others, but if we are inclined to make such judgments, should we not try to take everything into account?

One evening in the midst of the controversy, I was invited to be on *The Bill O'Reilly Factor* on Fox TV. The other panelists were a Southern Baptist seminary president and a Roman Catholic priest from New York, both anxious to condemn the president. Bill O'Reilly, the host, obviously shared their views. After some sparring, O'Reilly asked me point-blank what I thought of the president's character. In reply I remarked that my wife of forty-three years was in an adjacent room and that I had never done the kinds of things the president was accused of doing. Nevertheless, I said, "if the president were here I could not look him in the eye and say, 'Bill Clinton, I am a better man than you are.'" And, I added, turning to the others, "neither can you." I was reminding them, of course, that Christians cannot judge themselves better than others. Only God knows us in that ultimate sense. But having said such things, I immediately had to remind myself that I could not judge them either, or Ken Starr, or others in this troublesome drama. We have to judge actions and statements as best we can, praying that God will give us the gifts of wise discernment. But the rest we can leave to the One whose grace embraces us all.

Chapter Eleven

The Culture War

In which I am drawn ever more deeply into the American "culture war" of the 1990s, experiencing it from the vantage point of a Foundry Church under attack—participate in struggles at United Methodist General Conferences of 1996 and 2000—battle the temptations toward cynicism—wonder how to be tolerant of the intolerant—wonder how to help restore civility to a troubled land

The "culture war" of the 1990s really began much earlier. It was more or less officially declared in unsuccessful presidential candidate Patrick Buchanan's speech to the 1988 Republican National Convention—a speech that roused the faithful but helped undermine the elder George Bush's reelection campaign. The phrase referred then, and now, to the serious conflict over what shared symbols and values should define American life. It is about which symbols and values should be honored publicly and which should be rejected and stigmatized. The seriousness of the struggle has been magnified by its intrusion into the politics of the nation through efforts to enact laws prohibiting or protecting practices embodying the contested values. The culture war was not simply an exercise in public dialogue; it was to become a power struggle over how far the cultural life and practices of the nation should be governed by force of law. In that sense, it really was "war," although not generally conducted by violent means.[1]

Such conflicts are not new to American history. In my own lifetime the most important has been the struggle to overcome racism and its institu-

1. Such struggles, at least at the fringes, often do become violent—as in the attacks on abortion clinics and upon gay and lesbian people, with some actual killing.

tional expressions. The cultural aspects of that battle had to do with how race is to be defined, whether "membership" in a race confers superiority or inferiority, whether social contact among persons of different races is desirable or undesirable, whether intelligence correlates with race, and so on. Politically the struggle was over forms of racial discrimination required or permitted by law and whether the continuing effects of racial discrimination should be overcome through affirmative action. While it cannot be said that the struggle is yet fully resolved, there is now broad recognition among scientists that race itself is a questionable concept genetically. The changes over the past half century in these regards have truly been extraordinary, so that most Americans no longer believe that race confers superiority or inferiority or that enforced segregation should be tolerated by law. A culture war can truly have consequences.

The main issues in the current struggle include abortion, homosexuality (including recognition of same-sex unions analogous to marriage and whether gay and lesbian persons should be allowed to serve in the armed forces), sexual life and the degree to which pornography should be allowed in the media, the role of religion in public life (especially in the public schools—including the battle over teaching evolution versus "creation science"), the role of women, and drug policy. Underneath several of these issues there is a subtler question: Should morality be defined *prescriptively* (conformity to rules and principles) or *relationally* (expressing respect and love in relationship). Most ethicists, to whom the distinction is very familiar, recognize that both are important. Yet which has priority over the other can determine whether we understand morality as objective conformity to rules imposed from without or as a spiritual reality expressing love in grateful response to the grace of God.

Sometimes the culture war of our time is seen in sweeping terms as "conservatives" versus "liberals." Such terminology can be very misleading. For example a "liberal" might be one who is eager to preserve the Bill of Rights—essentially a conserving view. And a "conservative" might advocate radical changes in law to prohibit behaviors that previously have been tolerated. Moreover, a person can be very liberal on one issue, such as racial justice, while being quite conservative on another, such as expanding the rights of gay and lesbian people. It can be very difficult to identify the battle lines! I have often been classified as a liberal, and I do not shy away from that label. Yet there are issues on which I part company with many of those with whom I am usually allied. For instance, while I am opposed to prayer in public schools, I would support the kind of moment of silence the UN observes—provided this can be done in such a way that there is no implied state sponsorship of particular religious views. By some, the moment could be simply a time of reflection; for all, it could be a recognition of the private spiritual dignity of every student. Moreover, I part company with my pacifist friends by believing that military force must sometimes be employed to enforce justice and restrain evil. The lines can become blurred.

Still, there certainly has been a culture war! Organizations such as the Moral Majority, the Christian Coalition, the National Right to Life Committee, and the Family Research Council have been arrayed against the National Organization of Women, the Human Rights Campaign, Planned Parenthood, and the ACLU. Extremists can be found at both ends of the spectrum, embarrassing those who generally agree with their goals but not their methods.

Underneath it all, religion has played a major role. The Christian Coalition of Pat Robertson and Ralph Reed attracted large numbers of evangelical Christians seeking to reclaim "our culture" with effective political campaigning from local to national levels. The Interfaith Alliance came into being to challenge the implicit claim of the Christian Coalition to be the exclusive political voice of Christians—and to encourage political participation by persons of all religious groups. Robertson provided rhetorical ammunition for both sides with statements such as this one: "But let us not stop short until there is a complete restoration of the time-honored traditions of this nation, the complete fall of liberalism, and God's blessings are once again upon the land."[2] In many respects, the culture war of the 1990s seemed a replay of the fundamentalist controversies of the early twentieth century, including the famous Scopes trial of 1925.

The View from Foundry

At Foundry, we were drawn into this struggle almost from the time of my arrival. That was partly because of our internal movement toward becoming a Reconciling Congregation. By going out of our way to welcome gay and lesbian people, we offended those who were opposed to any acceptance of homosexuality in American culture. That might not have made us a particularly important target, but we were the church of some very high-profile people—especially the Clintons and the Doles. They could be gotten at by impugning their church. Then there was the person they heard most often from the Foundry pulpit! I can't imagine that my views

2. Pat Robertson, *The Turning Tide* (Dallas: Word Publishing, 1993), 302.

on any subject would have attracted much notice beyond the church apart from the presence of these national leaders and, to some extent, the church's location. But those views were contrary to the evangelical right wing at many points, and the church was favored with unusual attention by our critics.

Sometimes that took the form of Sunday morning demonstrations in front of the church. No doubt, most of these were designed to attract media attention, since the media were much in evidence when the president was in church. Some of the demonstrations were well mannered, mounted one might suppose more in sorrow than in anger. I remember one antiabortion demonstration of that sort. The group of about twenty were mostly Roman Catholic and were accompanied by a priest. They were circled in prayer. I joined the circle for a few moments, introduced myself, and invited them to come in for coffee at our fellowship hour following the service. They responded positively.

Other demonstrations weren't quite so friendly. We were favored by the presence of Randall Terry's Operation Rescue one Sunday, driving up in a bus emblazoned with antiabortion slogans and the usual pictures and with a loudspeaker blaring. The bus in fact had first gone to First Baptist Church, a block south of Foundry, on the mistaken assumption that that was the church attended by President Clinton. Redirected to Foundry, they set up their demonstration. (On this or another occasion, I was later told, Terry himself came into one of our services and was taken by the warmth and genuineness of the people.) The antiabortion demonstrations by Operation Rescue and others appeared to be directed at Foundry itself. But the curious thing is that abortion is about the only culture war controversy Foundry largely ignored during my years there. My own views on the subject, definitely on the prochoice side, were doubtless known by some involved in the demonstrations. But even though I had written a bit about the subject through the years, I very rarely touched on the subject from the pulpit. Perhaps I should have, but I didn't. Still, the demonstrations came.

One left-wing demonstration was mounted over a period of weeks by a group seeking clearance to ship computers to Cuba for medical purposes. Obviously aiming at the president, these demonstrators came to services over a period of weeks one Lenten season. They behaved well enough, announcing their presence only with their message on the yellow T-shirts they were wearing. Again, our congregation simply absorbed the group with hospitality. Eventually they were able to ship the computers, although I am confident that had nothing whatsoever to do with their demonstrations at Foundry.

Easily the most mean-spirited demonstrations were those of antigay groups, particularly Fred Phelps's Westboro Baptist contingent from Topeka, Kansas, who, I believe, protested twice at Foundry—first on the Sunday before President Clinton's second inaugural in 1997, and again during the weekend of the White House Conference on Hate Crimes. We had had advance warning they would be with us on the first of these occasions. They demonstrated first at the National Cathedral, and security at the cathedral informed us when they were on their way to Foundry. We were prepared, not with weapons of war, but with hot chocolate and donuts (and a sign to ensure that the media would treat this as a gesture of Foundry hospitality and not as Phelps's own supply service). The Topeka group had to share the stage that day with another demonstrating contingent from Operation Rescue, and I never did ascertain how well those two groups got along. I'm told that those to whom the refreshments were offered turned to their leaders to make sure it would be all right before accepting this offering from their presumed adversaries. Perhaps our hospitality was more a matter of shrewd public relations than of Christian grace, and yet we really did want to practice what we preach.

The other antigay demonstration (November 9, 1997) led us to a different response. Here were signs with unspeakable words about how God hates gays, some of them carried by young children, six or eight years old. Our people, as always, had to thread their way through this mess to get to the church doors. I usually thought it best not to dignify even a hateful demonstration by comment from the pulpit, and I followed that rule in the first service. During the half-hour between services, however, a gay man came up to me with tears in his eyes. Obviously affected by the hate outside our doors, he asked whether *something* could be said. I thought it over and concluded he was right. So I spoke to the congregation about the contrast between the hate outside and the love inside, about the rejection on the street and the warm acceptance in the sanctuary. But then I went further. I charged that the mainline churches share responsibility for the extremists by not being very clear about God's love for gay and lesbian people, as the churches slip into the language of condemnation. I said that through the centuries one of the great privileges of the church has been to share the stigma of rejected people, and Foundry accepts that vocation. The congregation responded warmly, and our daughter Jeanie applauded me, saying, "Dad, you really came out smoking with that sermon."

The White House Conference on Hate Crimes the next day provided a kind of postscript. The Phelps operation was there with the same signs, some carried by the same children, to greet busloads of conference participants as they arrived at the George Washington University auditorium where the meeting was held. And thus the demonstration provided a graphic illustration of what the conference was all about. President Clinton was at his best when he spoke to the conference about our challenge to make the diversity of America work and for this nation thus to be a beacon to the rest of the world. He spoke soberly of how meanness and hate represent a side of human nature that is always waiting, ready to emerge, and how we must strive to ensure that the positive side of our nature prevails. I thought that this is an especially serious responsibility of the churches. And I confess that it also gave me some pride that President Clinton had been nurtured and supported in those years by a Foundry Church that pretty much exemplifies the qualities he was commending to the nation.

Responding to "Christian Hate Mail"

I have already mentioned the considerable media attention paid to Foundry during those years. Some of the attention was simply factual, some was very positive, some was clearly an expression of the culture war. I would have to classify the Cal Thomas column of 1995 in that latter vein, along with unfriendly treatment in newsletters and other publications by organizations such as the Institute for Religion and Democracy, the American Family Association, and the Family Research Council. In fact, I believe we could have tracked the journalistic trail from an initial release by, say, the IRD, to other national conservative outlets, to Bible Belt regional outlets and smaller newspapers, and thence to individual believers, working almost like the food chain. Everything depended upon what was swallowed at the beginning. The end of the chain was often a nasty letter or phone call from some outraged citizen who had swallowed it all. My secretary and I started referring to this as our "Christian hate mail," with a certain amount of irony attached to the label "Christian." Here is a small sampling:

> This is an outrage! I strongly suggest that you read what God did with Gays of Sodom and Gomorrah, in the Bible. I am seeing red at the thought that one could stoop *so low* as to call Jesus a drag queen.[3] May God show mercy on your soul in Hell. . . . One day you will know

3. This refers to the dishonest report of a conference on ministry to gays and lesbians that was held at Foundry, which I referred to in chapter 9. The widely disseminated conservative news release on the conference generated a whole lot of mail in the spirit of the one I've quoted.

> when Christ says "Depart from me. I never knew you" unto everlasting hell. . . . Don't blame me. I didn't write the Bible—God did.
>
> I would suggest to you that you get on your knees and pray hard that the Spirit of God will touch you and change what you might become. If you are not touched by the Holy Spirit, at least create your own church and quit hiding behind ours.
>
> Leviticus 18:22 and Lev. 20:13 tells you that homosexuals are an abomination to the Lord—I Cor. 6:9 says they *will not* enter the kingdom of heaven. You are encouraging them to go to Hell when you condone their lifestyle. Their blood will be on your head because you are not speaking the truth to them.

That last letter concluded on a semi-graceful note: "Thank you for your time and thoughts on my comments. I pray for God to give you understanding that Satan is blinding your spiritual eye." In the words of the spiritual, I recognize that I am always "standing in the need of prayer," although I could probably get along without prayers of this kind.

At first I took such communications quite seriously and personally, spending inordinate time in thinking up the right answers and not trying to be too defensive about it. After the Rainbow of Life Conference letters began mounting up, however, I developed a more or less standard reply, including such lines as these:

> I have received your letter of [date] and note with sorrow your concern. You may well imagine my own distress when I reflect on the distortions, misperceptions, and inaccuracies in reports of that day, and I hardly know where I would begin in attempting to set the record straight. Let me assure you that we are a people who deeply love the Lord, who conscientiously study the Bible . . . and who strive to know God's will for our lives.

The letter concluded with the words, "Please keep us in your prayers." I was not thinking of being prayed for in the spirit of the letters promising prayers for me to mend my wicked ways.

No circumstances generated as much mail as the White House crisis of 1998–99. At first, as the volume of such mail increased dramatically, I concluded that this was a waste of time. Occasionally I would take a phone call or respond to a letter, but more often not.

Tony Campolo persuaded me that if at all possible one should respond even to hateful letters. Sometimes, he observed, you can make a real difference in a person's attitude simply by giving him or her attention in a positive spirit. Often, of course, there is no further communication, so there is no way to know how or whether you've affected somebody's thinking. And the particularly nasty letters are often sent anonymously. But, when possible, I tried to respond in a constructive spirit. One letter, from a fellow United Methodist minister in North Carolina, referred to some published comments of mine by saying that "the nicest thing I can say about this article is what a load of insinuation, double talk, innuendo and fertilizer." I'd hate to think what the unkindest thing he could say would have looked like! Still, I replied in this vein (after the president's acquittal by the Senate):

> Thank you for your letter of February 3. You would not be surprised to find that I cannot agree with much of what you have said, nor with your interpretation of what I have said. This has been a difficult time for all of us, and it may be the time now to take a deep breath and move on. My prayer is that the president's leadership and his personal actions in the remaining two years of his term will be such that even those who are disappointed by the Senate acquittal will, in the end, also be glad that he was not removed from office. Blessings on you in your minsitry. It would be good to talk with you sometime.

I did feel it important sometimes to correct misunderstandings. The "Caring and Sharing Sunday School Class" of a church in Florida wrote to say that "we strongly disagree with President Clinton's pastor and counselor, the Rev. Philip Wogaman, when he stated that sexual misconduct (adultery) does not constitute sin." I replied:

> I greatly appreciate your sending me a copy of your letter, because it gives me an opportunity to correct a serious misunderstanding of my views. I have not said, nor would I ever say, that "sexual misconduct does not constitute sin." It certainly does constitute sin. . . . It is painful to be misunderstood in such important matters, particularly if there appears to be a political agenda behind the misunderstanding. None of us can claim to have all wisdom and all knowledge, but we can strive earnestly to fulfill the most important role of all, which is to live in faithfulness to God.

Another harsh letter, also based on misunderstandings, came from a woman identifying herself with one of the Eastern Orthodox churches.

I replied to correct the record but also to speak of my understanding of the grace that is at the heart of her faith. I was touched to receive a reply in a very different vein, which she wrote with kindness and appreciation.

Still another letter, this one from Virginia, wrote to question my calling as a minister:

> After hearing your comments on *Crossfire* several nights ago, I cannot help wondering if you have made a good choice for your life's work. Have you not had some doubt yourself? Your comments surely do not sound like any minister I have ever heard.

I sought to reply with grace even to that. Privately and ruefully I had to wonder in low moments whether I *had* made the right choice of vocation! Mean-spiritedness within the church itself and in communications from other Christians can tempt one to be very cynical. Cynicism thrives, I think, upon the demonstrated powerlessness of the good. If the gospel of love cannot dominate the lives of Christianity, we ask, then what use is Christianity? I do not wonder that many give up on the church.

But the moments of doubt and cynicism were few and far between, even in the midst of the struggle. Carolyn was with me all the way with encouragement and helpful words of advice, and I was surrounded by a caring family and a caring church. I never really doubted that we were on the right course as long as we kept faith with the spirit of love. In addition to support from family and from the Foundry congregation, I received many communications from around the country that were very different in tone from the negative ones. A nice note from Ohio said, "I just had the pleasure of hearing you speak before the National Press Club (on C-Span, December 15, 1998). I greatly appreciate and commend you for your love, support, comfort, guidance and counsel of our dear President and his family during this extremely stressful ordeal." A Yale Divinity School professor wrote to say, "I am glad that you are doing the ministry you are. May God be with you!" A Californian wrote, "I understand that you are counseling President Clinton on matters related to betrayal and forgiveness. I heartily agree with your perspective on these issues, as I have felt touched to read your recent comments in the newspaper. It saddens me greatly that our society hasn't yet grown enough in wisdom and understanding to heal and forgive basic human frailties, even as we give lip service to the core Christian notion of love and forgiveness." And then a letter from Kentucky said, "This is just a quick note of support for you and the statements you have made in recent months regarding President Clinton, Christianity, and the Methodist Church."

There were many more letters, both supportive and critical. They gave me concrete, grassroots evidence of how polarized the country was. I sensed throughout the White House crisis that the issues cut deeper than the immediate controversy over President Clinton, that they had to do with more basic ideas and values shaping the culture in which we live. The passion conveyed by so many of the letters suggested that people were investing their whole selves in this national drama and its outcome. I wondered why many of my fellow Christians could not see this in relation to the deeper biblical and theological faith that we shared. My efforts to appeal to that common core of faith must have come across as clumsy. For some I was an adversary, for others an ally in a culture war. But most of all we needed to move beyond culture war to cultural dialogue with mutual respect and a recognition of our bonds of fellow humanity. In the heat of controversy I had to remind myself, again and again, that I could not express grace ungraciously, or preach love unlovingly. There was quite enough venom in the air without my adding to it. I know I did not always succeed. And yet I discovered that it is possible to communicate with people on a deeper plane, at least some of the time. I became more confident that in the end our society will see its way through, just as I think the common sense of most Americans contributed greatly to resolving the impeachment controversy constructively.

The Christian Coalition and the Interfaith Alliance

From its founding in 1989, the Christian Coalition quickly became a major force in American public life. A kind of successor to Jerry Falwell's Moral Majority, the Christian Coalition also emphasized a conservative agenda on cultural issues such as abortion, homosexuality, and school prayer, intermingled with support for less government, lower taxes, harsher punishments for crime, and diminished social welfare programs. Its original base was the mailing list of the failed Pat Robertson campaign for the 1988 Republican presidential nomination, and Robertson himself was its founder. Under the executive leadership of Ralph Reed, the organization was soon well organized and well funded at local, state, and national levels.[4] Its name and its rhetoric often implied that it represented the only authentic Christian voice in the nation's public life. It was widely,

4. Ralph Reed outlines the history and purposes of the Christian Coalition in his *Active Faith: How Christians Are Changing the Soul of American Politics* (New York: Free Press, 1996).

and I think rightly, perceived as a narrow and divisive new factor in politics, and one of the main forces behind the increasing polarization and mean-spiritedness of politics.

In response, the Interfaith Alliance was organized in 1994 to foster a more civil and inclusive conception of religion in public life. From its beginnings, the Alliance sought to include persons of a wide variety of faith traditions in its leadership. Its leaders and supporters included people with a wide variety of viewpoints on the main cultural issues of the day, such as abortion and homosexuality. But the unifying factors were conviction that religion should play an active and healing role in public life and that the public dialogue should be conducted with mutual respect and civility. Consequently, the organization challenged misleading and slanderous campaigning and the notion that only Christians, and narrow ones at that, had anything worthwhile to contribute to American politics.

I was attracted to the Alliance's purposes and, when asked in late 1994 to join its first board of directors, I readily accepted. Lacking the large financial base of organizations like the Christian Coalition, we found ourselves in a constant struggle for enough resources to keep our promising new movement going even as we reached out with our message. Since the organization was headquartered in Washington, D.C., I was often called upon in various ways to help with its development. In 1998 and 1999 I served as its president. That was a time of transition. In recent years the Alliance has developed a larger support base, with more than 100,000 supporters across the country and a number of state and local affiliates. A major source of support has been the active encouragement of the former news anchor Walter Cronkite.

As the Alliance evolved, I was struck by the fact that it was about the only national expression of genuinely interfaith cooperation. Its leaders included Roman Catholic bishops, well-known Protestant leaders (including the general secretary of the National Council of Churches and the presiding bishop of the Episcopal Church), leading Jewish rabbis, and Muslim, Hindu, and Buddhist leaders. Quite apart from its role in responding to religious extremism, the Alliance was beginning to provide a much-needed model of how very different faith traditions can find common ground in a diverse society. Those who are convinced that their own faith has exclusive possession of truth are not comfortable with such a vision, but the Interfaith Alliance was born out of great respect for different traditions. Like Foundry Church, it viewed diversity as a gift and not as an obstacle. Not surprisingly, the Foundry congregation supported my participation in ventures of this kind.

Church Struggle

Quite apart from the national political scene, American churches have themselves been a battleground in the struggle over ideas and values in this society. The struggle has been evidenced partly in the competition between more conservative and more liberal denominations—for example, between the Southern Baptists, Assembly of God, and Church of Christ, on the one hand, and the "mainline" denominations such as the United Methodists, Presbyterians, Episcopalians, and United Church of Christ, on the other. But the struggle also has been fought within and not just between denominations.

Even before going to Foundry, I was deeply involved in conflicts within the United Methodist Church. Beginning in the early 1970s I had written and lectured widely on the population problem, and I had written a widely distributed pamphlet supporting the Supreme Court's *Roe v. Wade* decision affirming the right to choose abortion. Gradually I became more involved in the homosexuality issue, as I've noted in chapter 8. I was elected as a delegate to the United Methodist General Conferences of 1988 and 1992, while still a seminary professor. At those quadrennial meetings I played a role in dealing with those issues and others.

At the 1988 General Conference, United Methodist theological statements were reviewed and revised. Much was at stake, for the General Conference is the only body that can speak for the whole church. Debate prior to the conference centered around the Bible. Would we, as United Methodists, declare the Bible to be "primary" in all of our doctrinal statements? No Christian should have much difficulty affirming that, but a whole lot depended on whether we would reaffirm the Wesleyan Quadrilateral referred to in chapter 7.

On the whole, those theological positions have stood the test of time. They have helped our church to transcend the hard edges of cultural conflict to a considerable extent. Several of us proposed some words, however, as an addition to the church's overall theological position: "We recognize that Scripture contains both authoritative witness to the word of God and expressions of human and cultural limitation." The motion failed, though by a fairly close margin. What I found interesting was that even those who spoke in opposition acknowledged that it was a true statement about the Bible—but, they argued, the laypeople weren't ready for that yet! Since for Christians a number of moral issues hinge on biblical interpretation, our proposed acknowledgment of limitations may have been more important even than we supposed.

After coming to Foundry, I also served at the 1996 and 2000 General Conferences. The big issues there centered largely around homosexuality and abortion. It seemed to me that the conferences were becoming increasingly conflicted. Although voting margins on key issues didn't change very much through the years, the adversarial spirit become more evident. The 2000 General Conference even witnessed demonstrations by people protesting the stance of the church on homosexuality, with numbers of people arrested. At that General Conference, I was anxious to help craft a compromise that might help heal the divisions within the church. Since the major question was whether we would continue to speak of homosexual practice as "incompatible with Christian teaching," I wondered whether we could adopt language that would acknowledge a difference of opinion on that question among people of good faith. This would be an honest statement of the situation and would acknowledge that our understanding of sexual orientation does not yet allow for sweeping closure on the subject. Efforts to effect that or some other compromise did not succeed. The battle lines seemed too tightly drawn, and the conservatives had enough votes to win without compromise. The conference did, however, adopt a statement that "we implore families and churches not to reject or condemn their lesbian and gay members and friends." To that extent there seemed to be a greater openness to the humanity of gay and lesbian people.

A bit to my surprise, given the cultural climate within the nation, the conference affirmed the long-standing United Methodist opposition to the death penalty by an overwhelming majority. And while there was an effort to adopt language speaking of Christ as the only way to salvation, that failed. In these and other ways, our church seemed to be positioned somewhere near the middle of the culture war. I hope we will, in the long run, help to heal it.

Why the Heat, Why the Passion?

Looking back at the culture war of these years, one wonders why it has consumed so much time and energy. Do the issues really matter so much? Has there been enough at stake to justify such passion?

Some issues do matter. Insofar as broadly shared values are implemented through law, people can go to jail for doing what is contrary to the majority's values. If, for instance, as a result of opposition to abortion it becomes a criminal act to perform an abortion, doctors can be jailed for providing this medical service. Even apart from law, insofar as passionate extremists are willing to act out their values and beliefs violently, doctors can be (and some have been) assassinated. Similarly, the cultural struggle over racism had to do, finally, with whether overt discrimination could be practiced in our society. People were being hurt. The large issue was whether the hurt could be removed.

I am struck at the spiritual level by the passion with which cultural struggles are fought out. I don't fully understand that, but I believe we can gain insight from the somewhat obscure studies of Ernest Becker.[5] Becker was impressed by the depth of human anxiety in the face of death. In their effort to surmount the threat of death, people often identify themselves with various human causes that they perceive to be lasting and universal. The success or failure of these causes becomes an ultimate issue for them, literally a life-and-death issue. Becker attributed the monstrous twentieth-century evils, like genocide, to this fanatical devotion to a cause. Having identified evil in human form, anything seems justified to stamp it out. Whether or not all fanaticism can be understood in this way, I find his insights helpful. Perhaps the truly religious response to this is through genuine trust in God who truly is eternal. Culture-war issues matter, but trusting more deeply in the grace of God can help us avoid demonizing our adversaries. We are then freer to look for points of agreement and more open to learn from others, so we can acknowledge truth on the other side, even when it might make it more difficult to "win." We can approach questions of truth more lucidly if perceptions of truth and error are not simply weapons of war. Above all, we will be less inclined to force the conscience of others.

I suppose the culture war will not end soon. Perhaps a large and diverse society is bound to have such conflicts perennially. My prayer is that churches like Foundry can be a source of insight and healing.

5. See Ernest Becker's books, *The Denial of Death* (New York: Free Press, 1973) and *Escape from Evil* (New York: Free Press, 1975).

Chapter Twelve

The Conclusion of the Clinton Presidency

In which the Clinton era comes to a conclusion, and a memorable service is held at Foundry, with the president preaching—I make some observations on the hectic last days at the White House—offer a perspective on the Clinton presidency and its effects upon Foundry Church

The end of the impeachment trial did not end the regular counseling sessions with the president that Tony, Gordon, and I had conducted since September 1998. President Clinton had committed himself to this process, and he honored that commitment through the remaining two years of his presidency. We continued to aim at an hour or so each week, with the three of us taking turns. On two or three occasions the three of us met with him together for a more extended period. Specifically personal matters discussed in the counseling sessions must remain private, of course. I can say that I felt the discussions were authentic, often from the heart, and they enhanced my view of Bill Clinton as a person and my respect for him as president. He was obviously working through a difficult aspect of his life, all the while seeking to be faithful to his commitment to the country to be an effective president.

I have already noted that I neither pretend to be, nor aspire to be, a trained psychotherapist—much as I value the contributions of that profession. I suspect, however, that spiritual counsel by a pastor makes similar contributions. Spiritual counsel has reference to our deepest values. It must deal with conflicts among values—or, to phrase this differently, the spiritual problems that arise when we are unable to keep faith with what is truly most important about our lives. It can help restore a deeper sense of self-esteem, based upon recovery of our true selfhood. Necessarily, it also deals with our vocation in life, what it is we set out to be and to do. For a Christian, this can be expressed as our response to the grace of God, God's loving acceptance of us despite our failings, and God's invitation to us to embody that grace in our lives with spiritual integrity.

Not surprisingly, all three of us made substantial use of the Bible in our discussions, and typically our sessions included a time of prayer in which all participated. Discussion and prayer often focused on the people who are affected by a president's decisions. I became far more aware of the dilemmas a conscientious president has to face, where any course of action will cause suffering and even death, and where one must struggle to make decisions that will do the most good, both in the short and long run. I think Bill Clinton really worked at making wise decisions for the sake of people who would be affected.

In some respects, the Kosovo conflict illustrated exactly such dilemmas. Here were tens of thousands of ethnic Albanians, forced to leave their homes and their country in a brutal exercise of "ethnic cleansing." Many were killed and many homes were destroyed. Could the international community stand by and watch these atrocities? The Serbian dictator, Slobodan Milosevic, was given every opportunity to end the brutality, but he would not. The decision to do something about it was not taken easily, but the president concluded that the well-being of the Albanian Kosovars and the long-term stability of the region and of Europe required resolute action. I am not equipped to assess such decision making, except to attest the moral seriousness with which the alternatives were weighed. I know how glad I was that I was not the one having to make such awesome decisions!

We were often in a position to give spiritual encouragement to people on the White House staff, and to see with appreciation how conscientious most of them were about their responsibilities. A number of these people had come to Foundry from time to time; some belonged to other churches and, I am sure, some had no church connections. We felt we could, in intangible ways, contribute something to their sense of personal worth and social vocation.

The Final Months

The approach of the year 2000 had rich significance for many people as the beginning of a new millennium. For the president, it marked the beginning of his last year in office. At a symbolic level, the Clintons seized upon the approach of the year 2000 to review different aspects of American life—what we could learn from the past, and what challenges and opportunities might confront us in the coming new millennium. Carolyn and I attended an East Room millennial observance, a lecture by church historian Martin E. Marty, and another, to us, very special event when George McGovern was awarded the Presidential Medal of Freedom. At the 1999 White House prayer breakfast, the president, with a few well-chosen words, had thanked the assembled religious leaders and the country for the grace he had received. The 2000 breakfast was a kind of valedictory to a similar group. Asked to offer the concluding prayer, I voiced the feelings of many of us with these words:

> Dear God, while breaking bread and taking counsel together, we have felt anew the bonds of our common humanity as your gift and our joy. We have gained fresh insight here into the problems facing the people of our land and other lands around the world. These are all your people, every one of them precious in your sight. Grant that knowledge may lead to deeper commitment, and commitment to greater service. We thank you for the leadership of the one who has called us here today, for his efforts to heal the broken places in our nation and throughout the world. . . . In these closing months of his administration, grant to President Clinton the continued gift of physical health and personal growth. And, when the time comes to lay down the burdens of this office, give to him and his family the love of a grateful nation and fresh opportunities to serve.

I was well aware that numbers of people in the country could not join in the latter part of that prayer, and so be it. Yet many could, including most if not all of those representing many religious faiths who were in attendance that day.

Those good wishes were clouded, however, by intense criticism at the very end over two issues: some of the president's concluding pardons and allegations that he was taking with him several pieces of White House property. I'm not sure such criticisms were all that well founded. In respect to the second one, I had personally witnessed his giving instructions to staff regarding personal possessions to be packed, and that where there was any doubt whether an item was personal it should not be taken.

Since I was myself supporting a presidential commutation for a federal prisoner, I had occasion to become familiar with that whole process as well. That commutation case involved the only person who had ever been prosecuted in the aftermath of the infamous Jonestown events of November 1978, when 913 people participated in a mass suicide or were killed. Larry Layton had been an idealistic young man when he came under the spell of the psychopathic Rev. Jim Jones. When Jones set up Jonestown in the jungles of Guyana, Layton was one of his chief lieutenants. Layton's involvement in the tragedy consisted of shooting two people at a jungle airstrip. Neither died, although several who had gone to Jonestown with Congressman Leo Ryan to investigate the cult were either killed (as was Ryan) or wounded by others. Guyanan authorities held Layton for a time but released him after concluding that he had been brainwashed. Back in California, Layton was later tried for participating in the conspiracy to kill Congressman Ryan and others. Juries were divided in the two successive trials. After the third, in 1986, he was convicted and, following federal guidelines, he was sentenced to twenty years to life.

I became involved in this case when contacted by a respected California clergyman who had lost loved ones in the tragedy. Despite his deep opposition to Jones, this minister felt that Layton's continued imprisonment was a real injustice. Later, the federal presentencing investigator in the case sent me a large file of relevant background materials and related that the federal district court judge in the case, now deceased, had felt that a sentence of five or six years would have been appropriate for the offense and regretted that he was bound by sentencing panel guidelines. The investigator himself considered Layton's continued imprisonment after fourteen years to be the greatest injustice he had experienced in several decades of work in law enforcement. Both the minister and the investigator, along with several others who had become involved in the case, urged me to join in seeking a presidential commutation.[1]

After studying the materials and talking with people involved in the case, I concluded with them that Mr. Layton's fourteen years in prison were quite enough. The fact that he had been a model prisoner and that he had violated no laws during the years between the Jonestown massacre and his sentencing underscored my belief that Layton's continued imprisonment served no good end. I wrote the president, calling attention to the petition for commutation that had already been filed and urging him to consider it seriously. In following through with this, I learned that there is an office in the Justice Department that routinely examines such petitions before advising the president and that there is also a staff position at the White House to process the materials for the president's attention.

1. A commutation involves a reduction in sentence, unlike a pardon, which sets it aside.

The president's chief of staff also plays a significant role. Several dozen petitions of various kinds were awaiting the president's final decision in the last days of his administration, and the list of pardons and commutations was announced on the very last day.

I gained new insight into the complexities of the process, and the inevitable confusions. The president was criticized for some of the pardons issued that last day, especially that of the financier Mark Rich. Some people raised questions about the presidential pardoning power itself. My own sense of that is very different, although I knew little more about the Rich pardon than I could read, pro and con, in the newspapers. Given the hundreds of thousands of inmates in federal prisons and the tendencies toward excessive sentences, and given the known instances of mistaken convictions, it seems to me that there has to be some avenue for executive intervention. There probably should be more, not fewer, pardons and commutations than any recent president has issued. I am also not convinced that the office in the Justice Department should have the last word. People in that bureaucracy have learned that they will never get in trouble if they say no to a petition! It can take an act of courage by a president or a governor to pardon a convict or issue a commutation, for, unlike the people in the Justice Department, these are elected leaders who are responsible to the public.

I was disappointed on January 20, 2001, to learn that Larry Layton had not made the list of pardons and commutations. I was later given to understand that the Layton commutation had been regarded favorably by the president. Evidently that piece of paper just wasn't in the pile of documents to be signed. Given the complexities and confusions of the process, and the understandable preoccupation of President Clinton with last-minute efforts to resolve the conflict between Israel and the Palestinians, I can understand how this particular petition might have gotten lost. I wrote a letter of spiritual support to Larry Layton, whom I had never met personally, and a subsequent letter to the parole board in California encouraging it to provide a parole. Some months later I was pleased to learn that that board, responding to the evidence and many communications, had decided to grant the parole.

Was it proper for me, as his pastor, to seek to influence the president's decision so directly? A president is constantly bombarded by requests from people. It can be especially refreshing and helpful to have relationships, especially with pastors and spiritual advisers, where that is not a factor. Where a pastor offers advice it should be very clear that the relationship does not depend upon its being taken, and, of course, one should not use this special access for personal favors. Such points granted, I feel comfortable with calling a president's or other political leader's attention to an issue of justice where he or she could make a difference. Morever, a pastor as preacher should not be inhibited from preaching on the issues of the day, so long as the views expressed have been considered carefully as an outgrowth of the gospel.

A Foundry Farewell

Several months before the end of his term, I had invited President Clinton to occupy the Foundry pulpit on a Sunday morning. As January 2001 approached, he accepted the invitation. He would preach at the second service on January 7, which also happened to be Epiphany Sunday.

Much as we would have liked to, we couldn't publicize this in advance, either in our regular ad in the *Washington Post* or in church newsletters. To do so would have risked having the church inundated with people who were not exactly attracted by Epiphany, as well as facing the possibility of hostile demonstrations and security problems. The White House didn't want us to give advance notice, and we didn't. I did cheat on that a little by advising church regulars, where possible, that next Sunday was going to be "special" and they wouldn't want to miss it. Of course, most church regulars could be expected to be there whether or not that Sunday was to be "special"! I preached at the first service and then informed that smaller congregation that President Clinton was to bring the message at the 11:00 service. This one time, I remarked, I would not be offended if they came to church to hear somebody else. Many did remain, and at the 11:00 hour the sanctuary was packed. Bishop and Mrs. Felton May also attended, and on this singular occasion we deviated from our usual rule by allowing photography, both by the White House and the communications office of the Baltimore-Washington Conference.

It really was a special service. The Scripture readings were presented by Hillary Rodham Clinton and by Chelsea Clinton, who had been active in our youth group. As he stood with me in the chancel during the hymn preceding the sermon time, the president whispered to me, "I hope I don't mess up." I thought that was quite funny, given his proven oratorical skills—and the fact that I had messed up often enough for both of us.

He greeted the bishop as "my good friend," and began by thanking the Foundry congregation "for being a church home to my family these last eight years." He thanked everybody for "your prayers and your welcome to all of us in the storm and sunshine of these last eight years." He continued:

> I will always have wonderful memories of every occasion where we passed the peace; for all the people, young and old, who came up to me and said a kind word of welcome; to remind me that no matter what was going on in Washington, D.C., at the moment, there was a real world out there, with real people and real hearts and minds. . . . You cannot imagine the peace, the comfort, the strength I have drawn from my Sundays here.

He commended the church for its social mission, its support of efforts to bring peace in the Middle East, Kosovo, and Northern Ireland, "where there are people suffering who have no money or power, too often overlooked by great nations with great interests." He cited Foundry's inclusiveness as a congregation and, in particular, the church's welcome "to gay and lesbian Christians, people who should not feel outside the family of God." He said other kind words for us, and then spoke of his life ahead. He cited former presidents John Quincy Adams and Jimmy Carter as models of productive life after leaving the White House and shared his hope that "in the next chapter of my life I will do my best to use the incredible opportunities my country has given me to be a good citizen here at home and around the world, to advance the causes I believe in and to lift the fortunes and hopes of those who deserve a better hand than they have been dealt—whether in Africa, Asia, Latin America or Appalachia, the Mississippi Delta, the inner cities or the Native American reservations." He remembered that "Christ admonished us that our lives will be judged by how we do unto the least of our neighbors," and he spoke of working for peace and reconciliation and finding ways "to get people to move beyond tolerance to celebration of [their] differences." He said more, concluding that "though we have all fallen short of the glory, we are all redeemed by faith in a loving God."

Eileen Guenther and the choir had prepared beautiful music, including the president's favorite hymns, "Precious Lord, Take My Hand" and "Amazing Grace." After Bishop May's benediction, the choir sang the beautiful "Gaelic Blessing," which ends, "Deep peace of Christ to you." And it was over.

Reflections on the Clinton Era

I have sometimes felt that it would take a Shakespeare to do justice to the drama of Washington during my thirty-six years observing life in this city: the events, the characters—some larger than life, some very ordinary—

the suspense, the crises, the adventures, the comedies, the tragedies. It has all been there. Nobody would dare invent stories approaching some of the things that have actually happened here!

Unfortunately, I am no Shakespeare.

In a more pedestrian way I ponder the Clinton years, in which I was destined as a pastor to play a small part. I cannot but feel that history will be kinder to this president than many of his contemporaries were. There is ample precedent for historical reevaluation. Even with those end-of-term flaps concerning presidential pardons, Bill Clinton ended his presidency with more than majority approval ratings from the American people. Along with that he has had bitter critics, some of whom viewed him with ill-concealed hatred. I am old enough to remember that when the now revered Harry Truman left office he was very unpopular with a large majority of the American people. Constitutionally, he could have run for reelection in 1952, but faced with evidence that he could not possibly win again, he chose not to try. By now there has been a total reassessment of the humble, plainspoken man from Missouri. Jimmy Carter, running for a second term, was soundly defeated by Ronald Reagan and had reason, then, to feel rejected by the American people. It is still too early to assess his presidency broadly, but he faced extraordinary difficulties, in spite of which he did things as a peacemaker that resulted in his belated Nobel Peace Prize in 2002.

I don't know what the historians will ultimately say about President Bill Clinton. Personally, I felt he grew tremendously in his feel for and effectiveness in international relations. He made his share of mistakes, but by the end of his second term he was the acknowledged leader of the world, and his leadership was focused upon global peace and improving the lot of the world's hungry and oppressed people. He was a president who worked very hard, bringing great gifts of intelligence and human sensitivity to that work. A side of his life proved to have been flawed, but the American people wisely did not define him in the end by the flaws.

Pondering his character and leadership, I've been impressed by two things. One was his sheer resiliency, a quality shared with his wife, Hillary. They simply never gave up. They had the gift of being able to keep coming back after reverses. I don't want to psychologize on this overmuch, but I suspect that quality in his case was partly the fruit of childhood difficulties he had learned to surmount. Many are defeated by such early problems; he may have been strengthened by them. At the root of that was a spiritual quality. Some have wondered—even to the point of asking me—whether his churchgoing, with Bible in hand, was only for show. Of course, any public figure is going to maximize behaviors that seem helpful politically. That is part of what politics is all about. But his churchgoing began, against considerable odds, when he was still a child, and it was nurtured along the way by a wide variety of contexts and personalities. I really think it is natural.

The other thing that has impressed me is his willingness to take risks as a leader. I'm not now speaking of the kind of risky behavior that got him into personal trouble, but of the political risks. His reputation among critics was of a leader who made his every move on the basis of public opinion polls, and there's no question he kept informed in that way. Maybe some of his decisions were too geared to anticipated approval, but when a big question arose on a matter that really counted, he was quite capable of running the risks. For instance, during the 1996 presidential campaign, he forthrightly opposed a popular measure on the California ballot specifying that English only should be used in the schools.

A personally risky action that impressed me even more was his decision to go to Gaza and address the Palestinian parliament—against the advice of the Secret Service, who understandably feared for his life. The night before that speech—about 3:00 A.M. Jerusalem time—he called and we talked a bit about the significance of the trip. My lingering impression was of his understanding of the importance this would have for the Palestinians and, ultimately, for peace. It turned out that the fears were unwarranted; he was met with great enthusiasm by the Palestinians. But he couldn't have known for sure that it would work out that way.

I have asked myself from time to time whether it was a pastoral mistake to devote as much attention to this president and, in particular, to give him so much public support. Some respected colleagues in ministry have asked me about this privately, and there have been some who have made that judgment in print, just as others have been supportive. There certainly have been religious leaders throughout history who have spoken "comfortable words" to and about powerful leaders when they should rather have spoken truth to power. Several of the greatest Hebrew prophets confronted kings with unwelcome truth they needed to hear. We do not much admire, in retrospect, those who have played the chaplaincy role too uncritically. Was I among them? I hope not.

In the end, though, I don't think I should be overly concerned about either those who criticized or those who applauded. What really mattered, as the Clinton administration came to an end, was whether I had responded faithfully and realistically to what was actually going on, both with the president and with the country. As a Christian minister, I have to leave the final judgments in the hands of God, knowing I will have to rely upon a good deal of grace!

Yet, looking back, I do not regret most of the choices made during those years. That includes what some might have considered the disproportionate attention I gave to the Clinton family during those years. It certainly was not prompted by the feeling that the president and first lady are of greater value in the eyes of God or more worthy of the pastoral support of the church. But in a very real sense, ministry to a president is ministry to the whole nation, indeed, the whole world. Helping a president focus on the spiritual dimensions of that awesome responsibility contributes to the president's vision of how to serve vast numbers of people he could never know personally.

My own role, especially the one I came to play publicly, was a burden, but it was also a privilege. Perhaps it helped reinforce the better instincts of many to know that a pastor who knew the president well considered him on balance to be a good man and a fine leader. Perhaps my preparation for this in years of study as an ethicist and theologian contributed something to the analysis of a very tangled situation. If in some small way it made a difference in helping the country avoid a bad decision at time of crisis, I thank God for that.

Chapter Thirteen

Endings

In which I face up to the fact that all good things come to an end—celebrate the year 2000—initiate a capital campaign and reflect on the dilemmas it posed for pastoral leadership—continue pastoral responsibilities—respond to September 11—help to plan services of repentance and reconciliation—participate in final celebrations and services

In its own way, the conclusion of the Clinton administration also marked the end of an era at Foundry Church. No question about it; the Clintons' presence had been a defining feature of those years. Some members worried. Having experienced the intensity of those years, especially on Sunday mornings, they wondered if the church was now going to experience sharp cutbacks in membership, attendance, and giving? One prominent member of the church spoke to me about this some months before the end of the Clinton presidency in exactly that vein, almost as though this was a large bubble that would burst.

That just didn't happen! No doubt there had been some increase in visitors during those years, partly by people who wanted to see the president of the United States up close and partly because of the church's increased national prominence. When in Washington, it might occur to tourists and convention-goers to attend this church they had heard so much about. Inevitably, that would recede.

But Foundry had been around since 1814; it has had a deep inner life and a solid core of very faithful members. Its inclusiveness and its overall character as a church would continue to be very attractive. In the end the statistics weren't much affected by the external change. Some people no doubt appreciated the fact that they no longer had to cope with metal detectors and other small inconveniences. There was a very small loss of members—1 or 2 percent—and a fall off in attendance at morning worship services of just a few percentage points. The church budget increased substantially during the period, even despite the onset of economic recession and a capital campaign. Those were the externals. The spirit of the church—its inclusiveness, its mission, its deeper commitments—remained very healthy and strong.

The Millennial Celebration

Even before the end of the Clinton administration, we had observed a significant landmark in time—the arrival of the year 2000. I confess I had looked forward to this for a very long time. Give or take a few years, it would be near the time of my retirement (if I should live that long). It was widely, though not universally, anticipated as the end of the second millennium and the beginning of the third. That, by definition, is something that only happens once in a thousand years, and we were privileged to be on hand to witness it.

I have always found New Year's Eve services—termed "watchnight services" in Methodist tradition—meaningful. These are times to take stock of the passing of the years, gathering up a whole year in retrospect and voicing our hopes for the new year. We had a small service at 11:00 P.M. on December 31 every year. These were usually in our small chapel, sometimes preceded by a party in the adjacent Helen Harris Parlor and usually concluded by the ringing of our lovely chimes at the stroke of midnight. That custom certainly didn't appeal to everybody, but for some of us it was a special time. Usually a handful of street people would wander in to participate, which brought an added dimension to the evening.

But now we could think some really long thoughts about past and future, now we could celebrate all that two thousand years of Christian history had meant for the world—along with some things to repent of, of course. So a year or two in advance, I began to promote the idea of a really great service for that special night. I even turned down a special invitation to preach at a millennial service in Singapore because I wanted to share this night with my own congregation. My enthusiasm proved to be slightly less than contagious, however. My original idea of a great celebratory service, packed sanctuary and all, and concluding at the stroke of midnight with the new year 2000, ran into three problems. The first was the understandable reluctance of numbers of people in the suburbs to come downtown, face the parking problems (we weren't able to secure our usual commercial parking garage), and risk the typical New Year's Eve drunken drivers. Some people just didn't like to leave their homes on New Year's Eve. The second was competition from a great projected national celebration with celebrities and fireworks on the Mall. And the third, I have to face it, was the fact that the whole thing was too much my idea and not enough something generated from within the congregation. Still, there was broad concurrence that this was indeed a special occasion calling for a grand worship experience.

We arrived at a compromise on the timing. The main service would be at 7:30 P.M., not 11:00, with a more intimate gathering to be held at 11:00 in the chapel for those who were as sentimental as I about the actual time.[1] Eileen and the choir pitched in to frame the night in beautiful music. Several hundred people turned out for the 7:30 service, and a surprisingly large group gathered in the chapel at 11:00. Our litany of gratitude gave thanks to God for the wonders of creation and the gift of our own lives; it spoke of God's presence in history, "ever speaking afresh through pioneers of faith, and through the poets and artists and scientists and leaders of every age, and through the unsung lives of those whose faithful service has brought us to this day." We proceeded to give thanks for the special gift of Jesus Christ and for God's presence with the church, "even in its failures of mind and will." A litany of confession developed for the occasion acknowledged "that the pages of our history have often been stained with sins, both of weakness and of malice," and that "the church has condoned and enabled human slavery, the subordination of women, the burning of heretics, the evils of racism and genocide, the tolerance of poverty, the stigmatizing of fellow human beings, the scourge of war." We acknowledged that "we have hurt those whom we should rather have loved and served, that we have sought to discover our own good in the ruin of [God's] intended good."

I had worked especially hard on my sermon for that night, having thought about it literally for years. Of course, the net effect of that was that I preached too long, especially considering the other elements in the

1. Of course this was all pretty arbitrary. By 7:30 P.M., earlier time zones had already ushered in the new millennium. Moreover, numbers of people—including my scientist colleague Walter—insisted that the actual millennium wouldn't start until 2001. Still, most of the world was captivated by the big round number when the world's odometer turned to 2000.

service. Perhaps I had an unconscious agenda to keep the service going until midnight after all! We stopped well short of that mark, but the experience reminded me that the quality of a sermon is not to be measured by its length. Still, I could speak about how that night was for us like a great prayer to God, of gratitude for how God had stood by humanity throughout the course of history with priceless gifts of freedom and love. And, following the words of Watts's great hymn, I spoke of God as "our hope for years to come," indeed, our *only* hope! We turned then to the age-old, central Christian sacrament of Communion. Then, as the service ended, we had a candlelight procession out into the night and a symbolic burning of confessions people had written on little slips of paper during the service, with several charcoal burners on the plaza in front of the church.

I did not attempt to preach during the second service. Several people had been recruited to read excerpts from great Christian voices of the past millennium, ranging from Francis of Assisi and Catherine of Siena to Martin Luther, William Penn and John Wesley, and then Frederick Douglass, Lucretia Mott, and Martin Luther King Jr. I couldn't have competed with them! We recited Walter Rauschenbusch's great prayer for the church, shared our hopes for 2000, heard from classic biblical passages of expectation, and observed a quiet time in which we could make our commitments for the time to come. At the stroke of midnight we exclaimed together, "This is the year 2000! Thanks be to God!"

It was a great night. I couldn't regret not having gone to Singapore, grand as that would have been. It was best to be with this congregation that had nurtured Carolyn and me and so many other people for so long. Here it was possible to think the long thoughts, despite the cares and distractions involved in planning and carrying out the services. It wasn't quite time for me to end my ministry, but it was a significant marker. I could look back on my own life as a portion of the millennia of Christian history with special gratitude for how God had guided and protected me. I made the point during the service that God's providence in history has not been so much through actual physical interventions but through spiritual nurturing with physical consequences. Certainly that had been true in my own life, at least insofar as I had responded to the nurturing. We could not expect God to come down out of the clouds to set everything right; we could anticipate and respond to the "still small voice" beckoning us to God's intended good for us and for the world. I resolved that night to do the very best I could for the remaining year and a half of my ministry at Foundry.

The Capital Campaign

Part of that had to be at a very mundane level. Foundry was not in bad shape, financially speaking. We were able to meet our obligations, expand the staff to deal with expanding opportunities for service (the staff was now larger than it had ever been), and increase the cushion of reserves in the operating budget. We had replaced the ninety-year-old slate roof with the same high quality slate, on the theory that if people ninety years ago were thinking ahead to us, we should be thinking of those who would come after us ninety years later. We had dealt with other deferred maintenance matters, such as repointing brick and stone, painting woodwork, and beginning the renewal of the old pews that we wanted to keep but that needed repair. All this and more had already been accomplished.

Still, I was concerned about the size of our endowment. Too large an endowment can make a church complacent, undermining the incentive to give, which carries with it commitment to serve. But a downtown church in a large city needs enough endowment to assure the long-term stability and security of its mission. There were enough examples of downtown churches in Washington and other cities that had come upon hard times and failed for lack of financial undergirding. Over the decades, churches have both "up" and "down" periods, and it can be fatal to come into a "down" period without adequate reserves. It is a little like the story of Joseph's interpretation of Pharaoh's dream about the seven years of prosperity followed by seven lean years. If a church cannot survive the lean years, it will soon be gone.

Perhaps it is sometimes a good thing when a church goes out of business. But given Foundry's history and its strategic location, it would be a tragedy for it to disappear. Not that that was or is likely at all, but I was concerned that we think of the long, long future.

So I had planted seeds in my annual reports for several years, and others among the lay leadership had arrived at the same conclusion: We needed to mount a capital campaign. The increase in endowment was to be a part of it. We also needed to take a new look at our old building. Could it be more beautiful? Could it be more functional for our mission? Could it be safer and more accessible?

Two matters of timing appeared to coincide. In the first place, the country was at the peak of unprecedented economic growth and prosperity. Many people, including many at Foundry, had benefited greatly from capital gains in the stock market. In the second place, I knew—though many at Foundry did not yet know—that I would have to retire no later than July 1, 2002, since I would have reached the mandatory retirement age of seventy that spring. It would not be feasible to have a successful capital campaign at the exact time of transition, and my successor—whoever that might prove to be—would need time to establish new leadership. It really had to be my responsibility to push this along if it was to begin before, say, 2004 or 2005. So we bit the bullet. The Church Council and the Board of Trustees made the decision to proceed. A consulting firm was hired. An engineering firm was retained to conduct a survey of the building. An architect was engaged for preliminary planning regarding space needs.

The engineering report brought the disappointing news that old electrical wiring and other infrastructure problems had to be dealt with soon and that the project cost would likely run between one and two million dollars. A feasibility study by the campaign consultants thought we might realistically aim at a goal of three million. The math didn't add up as we had hoped, but if anything the need was now more urgent. Notwithstanding building needs, we decided to keep the endowment as part of the campaign goal along with building needs, knowing that we could then seek loans as needed.

I confess I am not much of a fund-raiser. I had felt comfortable enough through the years in voicing the annual pledge campaign needs in announcements and sermons, mostly because I felt so strongly the value of this church and its mission. But making a general appeal is quite different from asking particular people individually for contributions—especially if one is asking for particular amounts. But that is exactly what the campaign consultants, and our own committee, were asking me to do! I was asked to talk with several major donor prospects, seeking pledges in the six-figure range, and then to sign letters to literally everybody in the congregation with suggested levels of pledging. Such appeals needed to acknowledge that the particular sought-for gifts might be quite impossible and that anything a person could do would be greatly appreciated. But I still felt a certain awkwardness about this. I'm sure the fund-raisers are right in that when such a campaign is mounted you rarely get what you don't ask for. Asking for particular amounts had a way of raising people's sights. I expect the pledges were higher, on the whole, as a result of the personal appeals and the letters than they would have been otherwise. Yet, as pastor, I did feel awkward about making such specific requests.

That awkwardness was increased by my receipt of some letters of protest, along with a bit of indirect reaction. One person even told me that he was going to give *less* than what he otherwise would have done because he considered the pastoral request out of order. Perhaps it was. Yet this led me to ponder a question: Why is it that a highly specific personal request from a pastor to a parishioner to *serve* in a particular way (for example, as chair of a committee or church school teacher) is accepted as appropriate even if it cannot be done, but a request for money raises questions? Does that suggest the unusual hold of money over our lives? A request for service is, in principle, not all that different from the appeal for money. So when one parishioner suggested I should apologize to the congregation, I couldn't agree to that. Most people did not seem to feel that way anyhow.

Nevertheless, and at a deeper level, I was concerned to hear reports of people who felt guilty that they were not able to pledge at the suggested levels. That was especially true of some older members who were already giving sacrificially. The requests, as formulated by the committee and consultants, were largely based on prior giving—so prior giving was not always a good predictor of the ability to give more! There was, I think, a pastoral problem here, and I tried to address it as best I could.

Our timing, in respect to the stock market's years of dramatic growth, couldn't have been much worse. We couldn't have known, I suppose, that the market would choose the launching of our campaign as the time for a serious downturn. Moreover, knowledge of my retirement date was increasing throughout the congregation as the campaign progressed. Still, all and all, the campaign was a positive thing for the church. It at least laid the foundations for further efforts. The lay leadership of the church was outstanding. Carolyn and I decided to make a large pledge that we would continue to pay for several years after leaving the church—we believed that strongly in the value of this church and its mission to its people, to the city, and to the world.

Ongoing Pastoral Responsibilities

Pastoral challenges and opportunities continued through the last year and a half of my work at Foundry. Deaths, weddings, baptisms, pastoral counseling—these things continue regardless of anything else. As a matter of fact, the longer one serves in a church of this kind the more the pastoral load seems to expand. After eight years I felt thoroughly bonded to the people, and that translated into many more calls for service.

Deaths continued to occur, some expected, some not. I have already mentioned Genevieve Taylor, whose death in fact occurred only half a year before my retirement. What a wise support she had been through the years and with what grace she had faced her time of death! Tom Hutchins was another whose death, while not unexpected, left a great gap in our church community. Tom was the strong, quiet type. His penetrating insights and sly sense of humor would come through at exactly those moments when you thought he wasn't paying any attention. In his last months he was confined to a wheelchair, a restriction he accepted with grace. Paul Daisey, who died at age eighty-eight toward the end of my pastorate, was another whose silence could be very misleading. When tempted to think he had drifted into something like Alzheimer's disease, he would surprise his friends and pastors with very lucid observations. Adele Hutchins and Annie Belle Daisey typified to me the surviving spouses of long marriages. Both are persons with deeply centered spiritual lives, but (if this is possible) both were experiencing a loss that is even deeper than grief. They, and others like them in the church, represent a very important part of pastoral ministry. I greatly regret not being able to be more helpful to surviving spouses, but clearly the Foundry community itself provides great support.

A very different kind of death occurred in late 2000. I had known Ruth Knispel almost since arriving at Foundry, but she was never in church. Almost completely immobilized with arthritis, she was confined to a nursing home in far Southeast Washington, except for occasional emergency treatment at a hospital next door. While unable to attend church, her continued loyalty to Foundry was quite extraordinary. She thrived on the weekly bulletins and any kind of communication she could get from the church. She had a handful of friends from the time she had been active in the United Methodist Women's organization, and she delighted in their visits and would ask me about them whenever I saw her. Carolyn devoted more time to her than I was able to, including being with her at the end of her life. One year, we had people in the 9:30 service take a moment to write messages on Christmas cards, which were then sent to shut-ins—a pastoral touch that I commend to others and wish we had done more often ourselves. Ruth received three or four of these cards, which she displayed proudly on the little bulletin board in her room for months thereafter. Eventually the time came when, at age ninety-one, there wasn't any more life in her. We had a combined memorial service for her and three other very old women, all of whom had died within a short period of time.

There were also some joyous weddings during those last months. Each of them was unique, but all of them were invested with hope and love. I continued to remind couples that there is no such thing as a perfect wedding ceremony, and that the main point about a wedding is the marriage. Despite its inevitable flaws and shortcomings, a wedding can be and usually is a happy celebration.

I felt the same way about baptisms. While we had some adult or teenage baptisms along the way, a large majority were of infants, which I especially enjoyed. Toward the end of my Foundry years, the numbers increased. Both in the prebaptismal counseling and in the baptism itself, I tried to embody the love of Christ and of the congregation for this precious young life. The precious young life did not always reciprocate, which sometimes gave the congregation a moment of levity. But we got along. For my last regular baptisms, the two boys who held the water vessel had been my first two infant baptisms ten years earlier. I took the occasion to remind the congregation that baptism is the preface to an ongoing process as the church assumes responsibility to nurture the young in Christian life. And here were two maturing young people who were visible evidence of that.

I thought these would be my last baptisms. In fact, however, there was to be one more. Following the usual midweek healing service for which I assumed responsibility, I spoke with a young woman who had a problem. She had never been baptized, although in her circle of family and friends it was assumed that she had been. For a variety of reasons she felt embarrassed to acknowledge this. After hearing her out and praying with her, I was prompted to ask: Would you like to be baptized now? "Oh yes," she said. I recruited a layperson who had been at the healing service. We went into the sanctuary, and I baptized her, with the understanding that she would unite with the church after my successor had begun his ministry. Normally, I believe baptisms should be in the context of a worship service. This was another exception to some good rules that one should normally follow.

Responding to September 11

Part of my work in the last year was responding to the searing national tragedy of September 11, 2001. I first heard what had happened at the World Trade Center and the Pentagon in a striking way. On Monday, September 10, I had begun preparation of my annual mission Sunday sermon. This year it was to be a focus upon our city, the greater Washington area, by means of the Metro rapid transit system. I would ride the entire system, carefully noting who got on and off at different points in the metropolitan area, the major institutions at stops along the way, the different kinds of businesses, and so on. I would weave this into an account of the city, its people, its problems, its resources. On that Monday I traveled the entirety of the red and green lines. Tuesday, September 11, I set forth to do the yellow, orange, and blue lines. Then I would digest all this and write.

And so it was that I stopped at the Pentagon station on the yellow line at approximately 9:05 A.M. Nothing remarkable there, not even many military personnel were in evidence. Still, I knew I would speak of this nerve center of the mightiest military power on earth. I proceeded to the end of the line several miles out in Virginia. Making contact with my secretary by cell phone, I learned of the first hit on the Twin Towers. Then, proceeding back toward the Pentagon, Sherie had more information to pass on. By now I was wondering whether I would have to change the subject for Sunday. Then Sherie called, pleading with me to get off the train because the Pentagon toward which I was now headed had been attacked. At this point the Metro was an elevated line, and from that vantage point I could see a great column of smoke rising above the Pentagon. The train stopped at a business and shopping center called Pentagon City, half a mile or so from the Pentagon itself. We were ushered off, joining the huge crowd milling around, looking for means of transportation. I wound up walking the five miles back to Foundry.

In memory, the next few days were a jumble of activity. We had a small service that night and a larger one the following evening, in place of our usual healing service. President Bush had asked houses of worship to hold services that Friday. Since we had already had two services, we decided not to. But then on Friday morning inquiries poured in: Were we having a service? Melvinia Brooks, answering the calls, logged in over 180. Midway through that we got our heads together and decided yes, we simply had to have a service. The staff all pitched in—Eileen planned the music, Jennifer Knudsen worked on aspects of the liturgy, I scrambled to put a sermon together, and Joe Arnold and Sherie Koob joined forces to get the word out and produce a bulletin. Somehow it happened, and the sanctuary was nearly full. There were prayers and music. My hastily constructed sermon was based on Isaiah, with its soaring words of comfort and hope at a time of Israel's great tragedy of defeat and exile.

The next Sunday the sanctuary was packed. It seemed like a Good Friday service with an Easter attendance. I had indeed changed my sermon subject, explaining the circumstances of my week to the congregation. Borrowing a title from theologian Paul Tillich, I preached on "The Shaking of the Foundations," with a text from Isaiah 24: "For the windows of heaven are opened, and the foundations of the earth tremble. The earth is utterly broken, the earth is torn asunder, the earth is violently shaken." Such language, I said, is very dramatic. Yet, I continued, "on Tuesday that would not have appeared extreme to those caught in the midst of the catastrophe." Our world, our assumptions, our illusions have been thoroughly shaken. "We all have a deeper sense of how vulnerable modern civilization is." But then we could turn to the text from 1 Corinthians 3: "No one can lay any foundation other than the one that has been laid; that foundation is Jesus Christ." Therein we rediscover that the real foundations of faith and love are also very much at work in the world. The crisis, while exhibiting great evil, was also the occasion for acts of courage and treasures of love.

Knowing the scope and proximity of the disasters and the size and connections of our congregation, I felt certain there would be people who had lost loved ones; perhaps we might discover Foundry members who had perished in the infernos. That Sunday morning, Sherie had gone over the complete list of those who had died at the Pentagon, which was published in the *Washington Post*. A name popped out corresponding to someone on our membership list. During the services I referred to her and to the brother-in-law of a Foundry member who had been working on an upper floor of one of the World Trade Center towers. When I asked for a show of hands of those who knew people who had died or were missing, numbers of hands went up.

There is a happy postscript to the story. That afternoon, after returning home, I called the home of the woman whose name was on the list. Only the voice mail came on, so I extended condolences and an offer to help any way we could, assuming that some relative would pick it up in a day or so. Two hours later, the woman herself called back! No, she had not been killed, but somebody whom she knew with her exact name had been. So we thanked God that she was safe, and in the same breath grieved the loss of her namesake who was not, along with all the others who had lost their lives.

In recent years Foundry has sought to avoid the false kind of patriotism that equates devotion to God with uncritical devotion to symbols of one's nation. Love of God must always come first, and that helps define the love of country. The September 11 crisis led us to reflect on that relationship. In the aftermath of that tragedy, I found it easy to invoke patriotic symbols, not as expressions of national power and glory but as love for a wounded people in its vulnerability. Even the patriotic hymn "God Bless America" took on a different meaning in this context. Often it is belted out as a kind of invocation of God's special favor to America among the world's nations, and when that is the connotation it is of course contrary to the deeper faith in God's equal love for all humankind—and in the underlying God-given unity of the entire family of humankind. But, seen in this moment of vulnerability, the actual words of that song are a kind of prayer for divine guidance through the night of our travail. Such an appeal is far removed from national arrogance. For a time, at least, the unity of the nation in its moment of vulnerability and pain represented, I thought, a deeper level of patriotism than we are accustomed to in this superpower. I am not sure we managed to sustain that deeper level of patriotism in subsequent months, but that is what we aimed for at Foundry.

A Time for Repentance

There was yet a piece of unfinished business long overdue at Foundry Church. Foundry has had a wonderful history in most respects, but there have been flaws as well. The largest of these was probably its treatment of African Americans in the early 1800s. Many persons of African descent, both slave and free, had been members of Foundry from the beginning. They were, however, treated with disrespect—often forced to worship in the balcony, denied leadership positions in the church, generally treated as inferiors. That came to a head in the 1830s, with the upshot that numbers of African Americans withdrew from Foundry, ultimately organizing Asbury Methodist Church nearby. While there continued to be close ties between the two churches, even shared ministry for a time, the racist trajectory continued through the years. As nearly as I could discover, Foundry was a thoroughly segregated church until the 1960s. Numbers of Foundry's old-timers had, in their younger years, sought to change that. Racial integration began to occur in the 1960s, broadening out in the 1970s and thereafter. Still, the history of discrimination and segregation remained.

When Dr. Eugene Matthews, senior pastor at Asbury, and I exchanged pulpits for a Sunday early in my ministry at Foundry, I resolved to say something about this to the Asbury congregation. Taking note of the history (of which most of the Asbury people were already quite aware), I spoke of how both these churches had gone on to be a vital Christian presence in downtown Washington. Nevertheless, I continued, we can imagine what it might have been if Foundry had been truly inclusive in its presence in the nation's capital during those pre–Civil War years. It might have made a significant difference. I concluded by saying, "I do not know whether any official representative of Foundry has apologized to you for that history, but I do so now."

The words were warmly received at Asbury, but something was still missing. Foundry's Religion, Race, and Culture Committee, interacting with a similar Asbury committee, planned some common educational opportunities, focusing on the realities of racism and attending to our joint history as churches. The result of this, during my last spring at Foundry, was a plan for Foundry to conduct a service of repentance at Asbury on a Lenten Sunday afternoon, and then for Asbury to conduct a service of reconciliation at Foundry the week after Easter.

There was initial resistance at both churches, particularly at Foundry. Many Foundry people rightly said they had had nothing personally to do with the shabby racism of the past. Indeed, there were now numbers of African Americans at Foundry. Should they, also Foundry members, participate in repentance for our church? The committee engaged in some very helpful educational activities, including efforts to educate our whole congregation about this history. I spoke of what such an event could mean, both from the pulpit and in less formal settings. I sought to help the congregation see the difference between repentance for what we have personally done or left undone and the corporate repentance of a community for the institutional sins of that community. The church had done serious wrong in the past, and we are now the people of that church. If we do not put a word of repentance on the record, we are through our silence condoning the history. That is particularly so insofar as we take general pride in our church's history.

The service of repentance was organized creatively by the committee, with Eileen Guenther's thoughtful assistance. We decided to hold it on Palm Sunday. By that day, our congregation was ready to participate wholeheartedly. It was a beautiful day. After our own morning services, many Foundry people formed a procession to walk the mile or so to Asbury. There we were greeted by Dr. Matthews and the Asbury congregation, who had prepared a lunch for us. Then we proceeded to the service. We presented a plaque with a carefully formulated statement of contrition that had been adopted by our Church Council, along with individual bookmarks embodying parts of the statement and a scriptural passage. Our choir brought some beautiful music, and statements were offered by representative members of the Foundry congregation. In my own remarks I commented that I wished the original founders of Asbury could be here to receive our repentance directly. I was confident, I said, that if the Foundry congregation and leaders from that time so long ago could be here today, they would want us to be their spokespersons in this act of repentance.

With this background, the service of reconciliation at Foundry the Sunday after Easter could be in an Easter spirit of renewal. This did not mean that we could all retreat into complacency about racism. There remains much to be done. But our ties with Asbury had become much closer through these services and all the planning that had gone into them.

Celebrations

The final months of our Foundry journey came with a rush. There was so much to do and so little time to do it! Pastoral demands continued unabated; if anything, they increased. Various committees had to be geared up for pastoral transition. I had to begin clearing out my office! That was a bigger challenge than I would have predicted. For one thing, it would mean finding increased space for a whole lot of books (even after getting rid of several hundred). I had to confront the fact that for the first time in forty years I would not have an academic or church office outside the home, so Carolyn and I had to engineer a number of changes in our house. (Fortunately, we had continued to reside in our own home through the Foundry years, since the church had no parsonage. At least we didn't have to move.)

We enjoyed the opportunity to interact with my successor, the Rev. Dean Snyder, and his wife, Jane Malone. It was clear that Dean was committed to the same basic values, including appreciation for Foundry's diversity and its being a Reconciling Congregation. He would, however, bring organizational and communication skills beyond what I could muster. A downtown church like Foundry, with a large constituency and mobility in and out, needs the continuity of long pastorates, but the occasional changes in pastoral leadership can bring fresh perspectives as well as new energy. Partly for that reason I trusted the decision-making process set forth in United Methodist church law, knowing this was not my decision to make. I was happy with the decision Bishop May and the cabinet made, after consulting with Foundry people; I was sure the church would thrive with Dean's leadership.

Toward the end, there were a number of farewell celebrations, including several given by church groups we had touched in this or that special way. Tears were shed by all of us, but Carolyn and I sought to use each of those times as a further opportunity to help the congregation focus on the future. Then came the last weekend, with a special Friday night churchwide dinner and program at a downtown hotel and a Saturday luncheon in Carolyn's honor. That luncheon represented the congregation's recognition of how much she had meant to everybody personally and how, in so many ways, ours had been a shared ministry.

The net effect of those occasions was to demolish whatever humility we had left after ten years with this wonderfully supportive congregation. We were touched by the gifts, including two quilts with special messages from individuals and groups on the different squares and a memory book artfully combining pictures and messages from many in the congregation. This last gift continues to evoke happy memories and reminds us that a pastoral journey touches the lives of people deeply. We were also greatly moved by a generous travel fund to which hundreds of Foundry people had contributed, which will enable us to do some very interesting things following retirement.

All of our children and most of our grandchildren were on hand for these final events. They managed, with smiles and wicked, but loving, asides, to help us keep it all in perspective. We felt surrounded by love of family and church.

The Last Services

The life of the church and of its pastors centers around occasions of worship. The final two services were very special. My next-to-last Sunday was Father's Day. I've never made much of that, but I took this one as a time to speak of how Jesus' reference to God as "Father" was an implied tribute to his own father. Had that not been a positive relationship, as it was in most Jewish families, the metaphor of "Father" could not have characterized the loving God. I made clear in the sermon that other positive metaphors, including "Mother," could also apply in the same way to God. For God, while beyond any gender classification, is spoken through human language as intimate and loving. But then, I spoke of my own father. He also had been a pastor, serving small-town churches throughout his ministry. He was a wonderful father, and his influence upon my own ministry has been incalculable. That next-to-last sermon was, in part, my tribute to him.

My last service was arranged by Eileen with consummate creativity. As she sought my advice about every detail it had something of the flavor of a condemned person ordering up the last meal. But I wanted it to combine the deep gratitude that Carolyn and I felt with a focus on Foundry's future. The title of my last sermon was "Endings," paralleling my first sermon back in 1992 on "Beginnings." The text was the passage in Hebrews 11 about how the great figures of Hebrew history had been men and women of faith who accomplished much but without seeing the final results of their work in the ever unfolding future: "All of these died in faith without having received the promises, but from a distance they saw and greeted them." So it is with all of us, I said. We do our best, trusting that God will take our efforts and perfect them, combining them with the faithful work of others in ways none of us could have dreamed. So our eyes can ever be directed toward that future. As we ended our work here, I said, I was confident that Foundry's best years lie ahead.

The choir sang a lovely Gaelic blessing as Carolyn joined me for the benediction. After pronouncing those words for the last time, I said "Go in peace. Keep us in your prayers as you shall be in ours; we have loved you very much."

Epilogue

So our pastoral journey was over. After gathering up the final boxes of odds and ends to take home, Carolyn and I went into the sanctuary. Empty now of people, it was bursting with memories. We could visualize many of the people, some who were nationally prominent, others of very low socioeconomic status, all with great dignity in the sight of God. In memory we could visualize people who had been a dynamic part of the life of the congregation but having died could now be numbered in what we have often called the church triumphant. We could see afresh the visitors who came each week from many other parts of this country and from abroad. I could look to the places in the sanctuary where Carolyn had sat and where I had always made eye contact with her before preaching, receiving her smile and silent encouragement.

We felt anew the energy of the sometimes hostile demonstrators, and the quiet grace with which this congregation had surrounded them. We could remember times of crisis, in both church and nation, when we had been able to draw upon a strength beyond our own to be the instruments of God's grace. We could recall our little errors that the congregation had somehow managed to overlook.

Together we knelt at the Communion rail to offer up our prayers of thanksgiving, our hopes for the church and its people, and to commit the work of these years into the hands of God.

And then we left, knowing we must allow space for a new pastor to establish his ministry and bond with the people without the complicating presence of his predecessor. But in leaving we were also committing ourselves to continue in ministry in other ways. Retirement from the United Methodist appointive ministry did not, in our view, mean retirement from ministry. That is commitment for a lifetime. In fact, the months following official retirement proved to be very busy ones, with a grandparents' camp with two of our grandchildren, a summer school teaching stint in Colorado, a weeklong camping trip with a son and grandsons in Oregon, several lectures, a five-week trip to Europe, a new venture in interfaith relations, and writing. The end of one journey is always the beginning of others.